100+ Rea FROM HO Gigs, Careers, and Side Hustles that You Can Do RIGHT NOW

Find and Keep a Job You Love Working Remotely

Full-Time, Part-Time, and Freelancer Work, Online & Offline

By

Rebecca Hurst

Published by:

Valley Of Joy Publishing Press

Cover & Interior designed

By

Lorie Robertson

First Edition

Contents

Introduction

I have always had several types of online work in place to earn extra income. I used those small hustles to create another type of work for myself online. You could say I am pretty resilient. No matter what challenges I may face, I always found a way to conquer them. If I was faced with a mountain of a problem, I usually found myself summiting it and coming off the face better for it.

In the regular working world, I have done many types of work. Lots of restaurant work, customer service, event staff, brand ambassador, catering, collections representative, general labor – the list goes on and on. I almost always have multiple sources of income because, to be fair, I have been a bit of a wild child and always needed a fallback plan.

The possibilities of work for me in the real world began to get slimmer and slimmer, I redoubled my efforts to create a steady source of income from online work. I was already doing book and product reviews, website data entry and research, and the occasional virtual assistant gig. A connection I had with the book reviews asked me if I was a writer. My first answer was no. Then I thought about it. As much as I love to read and as well as I did in school with writing. Why wouldn't I call myself a writer?

Thus began the real start of my online career as a home entrepreneur. And I love it. Navigating the maze of possibilities can be frustrating, confusing, and daunting, but it means freedom. Freedom from a fluctuating, ever-changing workplace. Freedom from working for one employer at a time. Freedom to make my own choices and hours. That freedom does come at a cost, as does as all freedom.

This book is one of those sources of income. In this book, I will explore the many types of online work available, what skills or equipment is necessary, how to make the most of your time and skills, how to find a real job working online today, and links to as many sources as possible.

Other books, blogs, and articles will direct you to the link to find the job, and then you have to figure out if it is for you. The goal here is to cut out some of that guesswork for you by supplying you with as much information as possible so that you can start your own process without having to wade through all the internet muck.

This book is set up in chapters divided by how you would go about finding a job you love. The first part is about finding what work you might want to do, establishing what you're good at, and general advice about job hunting and working from home. The bulk of the book is dedicated to practical guidance for finding that job in the real world. You can peruse the types of jobs that can be done remotely and how you might go about performing the job you love. Conversely, I have provided you with a listing of over 60 companies who are actively hiring remote, work from home workers.

Finally, I wrap up with addressing places to find freelance or gig work and suggesting some job opportunities you might take advantage of working from your house as a base of operations. While these jobs might not be done completely at home, you can still work out of your house without having to step foot in a cooperate office.

I hope this book helps you in your search for the perfect job for you. The reality is that we all must generate income in some way in order to live in this society, and you might as well do it on your terms with something you like doing.

Chapter 1: The Changing Workplace

Working from home is not a new thing. One hundred years ago, most people earned their income from their home or their land, often working and living in the same space. Blacksmiths, farmers, shopkeepers – they all operated some sort of business from their homes and the land that their homes were located on.

As the workforce became more industrial and technical, the workplace and workforce moved from being centrally located around one's home to another location. People started working at plants, mills, and processing centers –

commuting and leaving their homes for most of the 24-hour day.

When the internet exploded onto the scene in the 80s, the ability to work remotely gave a rebirth to the work from home trend. The more that the workplace adopted technology, the more people were able to work from their space at home rather than go into a physical workspace.

By the 2010s, technology had completely changed the workforce and workplace so that employees could more easily work remotely. Virtual conferencing, apps, updated software, and more easily accessible technology afforded businesses and workforce the ability to continue to grow the work from home industry.

As of 2020, there are over 5 million Americans working from home at least half the time, and that number continues to climb exponentially. The number of people working from home has climbed over 170% since 2005, and as technology growth continues to surge, the workforce will continue to adapt and grow with it.

For many people, myself included, there will be a massive amount of learning and adaption needed to be done to catch up with the changing world. Better to learn and change than to become obsolete and at a loss for options.

Is Online Work Right for You?

Let's discuss the traits and skills needed to be successful working from home.

Organization

Even when working for entities that have stringent rules and policies regarding their remote employees, it is still up to you to remain organized and disciplined in your work approach.

Communication

It is very hard to stay in communication with a boss, coworkers, clients, etc. if your communication skills are not up to par.

The written word and the electronic word lose some subtle nuances that voice inflection and body language help to convey.

Time-Consciousness

For the roles that involve a set schedule and hours, you will simply need to be mindful of a work-life balance that ensures you are ready to work on time.

In the roles where you work on projects, have to meet deadlines, or work on several tasks at once, you will need to have great time management skills in order to stay focused and on time.

Proactiveness

The best offense is a good defense. This means that you have to be looking ahead and planning for what comes next all the time.

Tech Savvy

One of my biggest challenges. Just because I love to read and write fairly well, does not mean I have a clue how to operate even a fraction of the latest technology. It becomes very necessary to be very techie fluent when working from home because you are literally always using technology.

Balance

To be successful, healthy, and happy, you have to have a proper work-life balance. There has to be time set specifically for work so that your personal time is not overwhelmed with worries about what was left undone and vice versa. This can be one of the hardest to achieve when working from home because work and home are one and the same.

What Do You Want to Do?

Just like in the 'real' world, there are many different types of online work. The more skilled you are, the more services you have to offer, therefore the more valuable and marketable you are to ant business, whether it is in person or online.

A high paying job with incredible benefits is normally only available to someone who has invested the time and effort to obtain a degree or to develop some kind of skill. Their level of knowledge and abilities makes them a greater asset to whatever company they are trying to get hired with.

Another parallel that the online working world has to the regular working world is the many types of work that are available. Part-time, full-time, temporary, contract, freelance, and self-employed are the different kinds of work available to people, whether it is in person or online. These terms are only in reference to the length of work, as in the number of hours being worked, and how the individual is being paid.

Additionally, online work has a few more words to convey the type of work being done. Telecommuting, telework, mobile work, and remote work are also words used to describe working from a computer from home.

For some individuals, the most comfortable, secure type of position is a full-time job with a large established company that offers a competitive wage in line with their skillset and good benefits for them and their families.

For others, more flexibility and multiple sources of income are more in line with their needs and lives. If this is the case, there are many options available. This is where all of the terms mentioned above come into play, and it is important to know the difference between each kind of work.

Part-time and full-time work both mean the same online as they do in person. The individual is working for a company, employed by that company, where taxes are taken out of their payment, as well as whatever benefits are being offered and utilized. Part-time and full-time work is self-explanatory. Part-time means you are working one to thirty hours per week and subject to whatever policies and rules the employer has in place for that type of position. Full-time entails working thirty-plus hours per week with any applicable benefits that were being offered. Almost all major companies have employees who work remotely. This is where skills, knowledge, and opportunity start to work hand in hand.

For those just starting out in the online work world and deciding what route to take, it is like all other things in life, it is best to educate yourself before making any decisions. Again, the core types of online work are contract, remote, freelance, and self-employed.

Contract Work

Contract work can encompass a variety of positions performing a variety of tasks. What they all have in common is that the person is not considered to be an employee of the company that they are working for and that the position is not considered permanent. In addition, the contract employee is paid the agreed-upon wage, benefits are normally not part of the offer, and there are no taxes taken out of their pay.

Remote Work

Remote work is any type of work that is done for an individual or company, but the tasks are performed from home or from a remote location. Whether the individual is working from home for a Fortune 500 company with a fantastic income with benefits or they are banging away at the computer on McDonald's free wi-fi, both parties are working remotely.

Freelance Work

Freelance work is like contract work in that the person works for a company or individual on a temporary basis for an agreed-upon wage, for a length of time to be determined by both the employee and the employer. The difference in the two terms is that the phrase contract work can be referred to both online and in-person work, and freelance is generally used more often to describe someone who does various online work on a contract basis.

Self-Employed

Self-employed individuals work for themselves. Whether they are doing landscaping, cleaning houses, creating websites, or acting as a YouTube channel host, these types of positions are often done on a self-employed basis. This means, that like the other positions listed above, the roles are varied, the length of time will change for each assignment, and there are no taxes to be taken out of their pay. That is something that self-employed people must handle on their own with the IRS.

While these terms are all very similar and can be interchangeable, there are advantages and disadvantages to each kind of work. It all comes down to what type of work you will be doing, what your needs are, your skillset, amount of time you can devote to the job, and other factors.

Chapter 2: Financial Considerations

One of the first things to consider when deciding what type of online work to pursue is financial considerations. In a regular job, there are several factors to consider.

Is there a commute from your home to the job site? How long does this commute take? What is the estimated maintenance for your vehicle for this commute? How much of your paycheck will go towards getting you back and forth to work? Do you have to wear a uniform? Is this uniform provided, or do you have to supply it? Can you bring your lunch? How often will you end up dining out?

The list goes on and on. Here in the Houston, Texas area, many people are very familiar with the fact that the commute is the first thing that you have to consider when thinking about a potential new job because it can be the one factor that makes the job completely unviable.

The same principle applies when you start a career online. First things first. Let's talk about money. Income is the reason that pretty much everyone goes to work. Without a source of income, most people are not able to maintain a decent standard of living for themselves and their families. So, the very first thing to consider is how much money do you need to make and how much time do you have to devote to pursue that income?

Online income is the same as any other income. The better you are at something, the more specialized your skill, the more that you get paid. For instance, a doctor who went to school for eight to ten additional years after high school is going to make way more money than someone with a GED with minimal job training.

That is just the way of the world. No getting around it. No passing go and collecting the easy two hundred bucks. If you want to jump right in making the most amount of money possible, you will need to get some sort of education or training that makes you more valuable.

Without that specified training or skill, there are still other options available. If you can read, write, type, and navigate the internet, there is something you can find to do online that will create a source of income. Personally, my advice would be to investigate several types of online work and utilize a couple of them. That will allow you more freedom as you find your niche, your spot in the online work world.

Keeping Track of Taxes

In a traditional work environment, varied as they are, the employee fills out paperwork upon hire, their hours are kept track of, and then they are issued a check at the end of the pay period. By the time the paycheck is issued, the employer will already have calculated and withdrawn the appropriate amount of taxes and sent them to the designated agencies.

When you are working as any type of employee where the taxes are not taken out. As a contractor, freelancer, self-employed, etc. person, the taxes are not automatically withdrawn, and once you have earned more than $600, you are responsible for ensuring that the proper amount of taxes have gone to the proper entities.

On a side note, if you are being paid without having registered all of your personal information, such as full name, date of birth, social security number, etc. then there is no way for anyone to track those monies. For example, employee John Doe goes to work for Company ABC. From the beginning, he provides all his personal information: date of birth, license number, address, social security number, etc. So, when it is time to be paid, Company ABC issues the pay, reports to the proper authorities, and sends in the correct payments.

Conversely, Jane Doe agrees to work for Company DEF as a freelancer. Company DEF only knows Jane Doe by her online name, "janedoeswebsites@website.com," and therefore has no tracking or personal identification information for her. They come to an agreement about what services will be performed and for what pay. Once the services have been rendered, Company DEF then sends a direct deposit into Jane Doe's PayPal account. Because the company did not have any personal identification information, there is literally no way for them to file anything with the IRS indicating who they paid these funds to. It is now up to Jane Doe how she chooses to report or not report those monies.

The point of this comparison is not to tell you not to file your taxes, but to let you know that once you are in control of your own taxes, everything is up to you. Including the consequences. The IRS is not an entity to play with, and it is important that you keep track of your income and be sure to send in the proper amount of taxes to the federal government and the state, where applicable to avoid any legal complications.

Considering Startup Costs

The startup costs to find real work from home jobs will be as varied as the jobs themselves. A functioning laptop, some amount of internet access, and electricity seem like the bare minimum to work from home. From there, it ranges to having a complete in-home office with hard-wired internet, a dedicated distraction-free workspace, extra monitors, headsets, webcams, software, specific download, and upload speeds and other variations depending on the specific employer.

Many of the jobs that are performed over the phone involve some level of customer's personal information being exchanged. These types of jobs, for the most part, will require that you have a few basic requirements. By basic, I simply mean a core set of requirements. Because basic could imply that these requirements are easy to attain, and that is not always the case. For most phone jobs, you will need to have (at least):

- A laptop three years old or newer
- Hard wired internet
- Headset
- Software
- Dedicated space in the home
- Monitor of a specified size

The amount of money needed to obtain these items are as varied as the jobs themselves and the people performing these jobs. The fact of the matter is that you will need some startup funds.

Later in this book, non-phone jobs will be covered in detail. While those jobs typically require much less equipment, there will be some basic things that you will need. All jobs from home require an internet connection. Otherwise, how will you connect with the world? A laptop is also a must. When you are not working on the phones, you can generally get away with any functioning laptop, so long as you have whatever skills are necessary to perform the tasks of the work. However, these are the very bare necessities and will only go up from there.

The bottom line is that startup costs range from however much your internet costs you to over a thousand dollars to create a fully functioning office environment. Thoroughly investigate whatever position you choose to take on before making any investments.

Chapter 3: Precautions

Here are some common pitfalls to avoid that most people who work from home may experience.

- Too many subscriptions to different types of 'help' or marketplaces to find gigs
- Investments into equipment for a job that will not develop a return
- Scammers who are trying to obtain your information for the purpose of fraud

Ways to Avoid a Negative Experience

For the most part, there are some general 'rules' that you can follow to avoid any negative experiences when trying to create an income that you can generate from home:

- Stay away from direct sales or multilevel marketing. Sales is a component for many phone-related jobs in the work from home field, but if you are not making an hourly wage and then some sort of commission, you may want to sidestep that 'opportunity.' MLM (multilevel marketing) has its own time, place, and purpose, or so they say – but for the purposes of working from home as a real job, not a great option.

- Stay away from pyramid schemes. Anything that requires you to get others to sign up is generally not a good idea. Hence, the pyramid concept.

- Carefully research businesses that require a startup kit. There will be some investment required on your part for a lot of work from home enterprise. This type of expenditure should be for your own equipment, computer, headset, monitor, etc. and not some sort of kit that the hiring entity requires you to purchase to get started. The only exception to this would be for those people who decide to pursue some sort of affiliate marketing or product sales. Those opportunities should be carefully researched before getting involved in them.

- Check cashing or money wiring – just don't do it.

- Home assembly or envelope stuffing. This is generally not a good idea. There may be a legitimate opportunity to make a little cash, and I do mean little, but for the most part, not a good idea.

- Products re-seller or wholesaler. I am not against being an affiliate marketer, eBay seller, Etsy shop owner, or any other venture where you essentially are creating your own business.

There are many, many scams and misinformation out there when it comes to selling any sort of product, so be very careful.

Signs of a Scam

I am naturally suspicious and skeptical via both nature and nurture, so I feel like I can smell a scam a mile away. For those who see the world with less scrutiny, a few tips on how to fall victim to a scam for either your information or your money:

- It pays too much for too little work. The truth is that online money is not easy money, so let that be a sign.

- The post/ad is not specific. There is some sort of opportunity that is available only to you that's going to make you rich overnight, but what you're doing is not specified. Just click here, send your email to get started today. Ignore it.

- Rags to riches instantly. If it sounds too good to be true, it probably is.

- Grammatical or spelling errors. If the ad or post itself has glaringly obvious errors, that's usually a bad sign.

- Immediate job offer. If you are offered the position/opportunity without any kind of qualifying interview, reference check, or online onboarding.

Chapter 4: Finding the Right Job for You

FINDING YOUR SKILLSET

Ever heard the saying, "Do what you love, and you'll never work another day in your life"? Realistically, there is a need, a necessity for work, and you won't always love it. I always prefer the ugly truth to a pretty lie, so let's just keep it real here and be honest.

For most of us, money is a necessity, and while we don't all love what we do, it is very favorable to at least enjoy it and be comfortable while not having to be constantly stressed out.

So, to find what the right type of work is for you, ask yourself a few questions:

- What are your passions? What do you love doing?

- What are your skills? What can you already do well? What can you do to enhance the skills you already have? Are there new skills you can learn?

- What is your previous experience? It is much easier to build on something you already have, but don't be afraid to try something new.

- Do you need health insurance? This is a very practical concern, especially for those with others who depend on them.

- What are your scheduling needs? Does it have to be flexible, or can you commit to a regular schedule? Just because you're at home doesn't mean you won't be on a schedule of some kind.

- Are you working on long term goals or meeting short term needs? Do you need to pay the light bill, or are you thinking of your kids' college funds?

- Do you want to start a business? If you want to start a new business, should you be focusing on earning a paycheck?

- What is your investment ability level? How much do you have to invest in equipment, internet, and other equipment to be able to start working at home?

- Are you able to and interested in furthering your education for more opportunities? I very highly recommend this option, and yes, I am taking my own advice here, too.

Types of Skills You May Have

There are three types of skills that pertain to most types of work: technical, measurable, and soft.

Technical Skills

These skills are often obtained through education and on the job training. Technical skills include the ability to build a cabinet, operate equipment, develop a website, sell products to customers, or write computer code.

Measurable Skills

A measurable skill is one that can be defined. I can type 65 wpm with 100% accuracy.

That is a skill that can be measured and defined.

Soft Skills

Soft skills are more like personality and character traits. They are more related to how you think, behave, and how you present yourself.

Being on time, a quick learner, and effective communicator are all examples of soft skills.

Evaluate Your Skills

From these examples of skills, what do you already have, what can you work on more, and what new skills can you learn?

Ways to assess your skills and what growth you can coax from yourself:

Reflect on your previous job descriptions.

For your current or last job, think about what tasks you were proficient in and then expand from there. For example, if you are an Excel aficionado, be specific with what exactly you can do. It is one thing to say you are a master at excel, it is another to be able to quantify and qualify exactly what you can do with Excel (or any other set of tasks).

Look at your past performance reviews.

What did your past employers have to say about your work? Use this to correct any mistakes and multiply your strengths

Ask other people for feedback.

Constructive criticism is not always easy to take, especially when it's not constructive, but it will help you to see yourself more clearly.

Revamp your resume.

Use the collection of information you gathered to revamp and revive your resume. Unless you're starting your own business, you're definitely still going to need a resume, even more so now that your dazzling personality can't be felt in person.

Take an online behavior test.

Try the DISC or Myers-Briggs tests to help you understand your personality traits, emotional intelligence, and identify your strengths and weaknesses.

Understanding Yourself

Working from home does not mean that you no longer have to interact with other people. No matter what the position is, there is always a level of human interaction that has to take place, even if the interaction is only electronic in nature.

Understanding yourself and knowing your strengths and weaknesses can be very helpful in your success as a person and as an employee/entrepreneur/business owner. Not only will it help your success quotient when it comes to making money, but it will also help with your personal relationships.

Try taking a personality test and see if the results ring true with who you know yourself to be:

https://www.truity.com/test/type-finder-personality-test-new

This free version is an offshoot of the Myers - Briggs indicator test. This self-administered questionnaire helps to identify the personal psychological preferences and how that changes the way people perceive the world, interact with other people around them, and then make their individual decisions.

Evaluating your personality type will not change who you are, your circumstances, or the type of work available to you right at this moment. However, it can help you to see opportunities that you might not have thought possible before. Or, it can help you to understand why certain types of work environments make you uncomfortable or less productive.

Chapter 5: 35 Real Work from Home Jobs

There is a plethora of jobs/tasks to do to earn money from home. The list was created with the intention of offering as much information as possible. What may sound crazy to you may work out great for someone else. Each type of job is ordered to give you an A-Z list of what money-making opportunities are available.

Then, each type of job is defined, the duties explained, any other pertinent information offered, and most importantly, a link (or a few) depending on what is available for each possibility, along with a description of what that entity is looking for.

There are multiple links posted for each type of job because different entities are seeking work from home assistance and varying times. This way, you will have many options to assist you in your search.

Each link was visited and verified to have a work from home opportunity available as of April 2020.

If there was a type of job left out or a site not listed, then either this author was not aware of the information, or at this time, the information was unavailable. For this instance, I offer my sincere apologies.

Affiliate Marketing	Art or Creative Services	Blogging	Book Reviewer
Chat Agents	Customer Service Representative	Closed Captions	Consulting
Data Entry	Editing and Proofreading	E-Commerce	Email Support
Graphic	Moderation	Music	Online

Designer			Poker
Podcasts	Programming	Telenursing/TeleDoctor	Research and Fact-Checking
Resume Writer	Reviewer	SEA/SEO Expert	Social Media
Teaching	Test Grading	Transcriptionist	Translation
Travel Agent	Typing	Video Editing	Virtual Assistant
Voice	Website/App Testing	Website Rating	Writing
Academic	Content	Copywriting	YouTube

Affiliate Marketing

This is performance-based marketing in which an individual earns a commission for marketing another person or company's products or services. The product or service owner can increase sales and traffic toward their product/service when the 'affiliate' helps to drive sales towards that product or service, in the interest of earning a commission. In turn, the affiliate can earn a commission without having to take on the cost or the labor incurred when selling products online or from providing the service themselves.

There are many, many affiliate programs hosted by a wide range of businesses, websites, and individuals. The products and services available for sale and affiliation also run the gamut in variety. Each entity that offers an affiliate venture will have different rules, policies, earning possibilities, and many other variables to consider. Thoroughly research all your options before making any choices and investing any time, effort, or expense.

Some of the top/most popular companies to be an affiliate for:

Amazon - https://affiliate-program.amazon.com/

Bluehost - https://www.bluehost.com/affiliates

Clickbank - https://accounts.clickbank.com/marketplace.htm

eBay - https://partnernetwork.ebay.com/

Target - https://affiliate.target.com/

Art or Creative Services

An artist is someone who is engaged in an activity related to creating art, practicing the arts, or demonstrating an art. The visual artist or creative person who works from home could practice their art under many different titles in a variety of roles.

The kinds of jobs an artist might find themselves doing when working from home include:

- Art teacher
- Graphic Designer
- Illustrator
- Storyline developer
- Photographer
- Logo Creator
- Layout Specialist

A few links to help guide you down the artistic path:

Cricket Media: http://cricketmedia.com/art-submissions/ Does not accept photography. Do not send original artwork because the art submissions will not be returned.

Edge science fiction and fantasy:

http://www.edgewebsite.com/artwork.html Looking for submissions for artwork for book covers and book jackets for science fiction and fantasy publishing.

Funny Times:

https://funnytimes.com/about/submissions/#.T9V XL9VSRjZ Accepts cartoon and short story submissions for funny cartoons about politics, news, relationships, food, technology, pets, work, death – nothing is off-limits.

Wild Apple: https://wildapple.com/submit/ This site is looking for talented artists that can be licensed and published. Specifically, they are looking for painters, photographers, illustrators, and artists who can create a story with an art collection.

Blogging

A blog is a regularly updated website or web page, typically run by an individual or small group, that is written in an informal or conversational style. Blog websites are typically oriented towards a single topic. Sharing information with the world via a website or web page is a beautiful thing. So, how do you make money with blog writing?

- Monetization through CPC (cost per click) or CPM (cost per thousand impressions) ads placed strategically on the site where the blog is located.

- Using the blogging platform to be an affiliate and including affiliate links on the website. This one way to use affiliate marketing to make money, as we previously discussed.

- Selling digital products for a commission or markup.

- Selling memberships to various organizations for commission. For example, you could write an article that can be tied to AARP. When the reader buys a membership to AARP, then the blogger receives some sort of commission for that sale.

Creating a blog on a website, establishing a following, and then earning money as a blogger is a time and money investment. A successful blogger would need to treat their blogging as a startup business rather than a hobby or a side venture to see any real money from it.

To get started as a blog writer is simple.

1. Pick a blog name. Choose something that represents your brand. You might also want to make sure that you can get the .com of your chosen name.

2. Get your blog online. Register your blog via any website or blog creator site. Some places you could start include Wix.com, WordPress, and Blogger. You can easily use these sites to customize your look.

3. Write and publish your first post. You should have a clear audience in mind that matches your brand and what topic you want to write about. I would also say that you should limit your topics to a specific focus. Most readers will be drawn to your blog because they are looking for a certain post about a particular subject. Your readers should know what to expect.

4. Post regularly and often. You should post at the same time each day if you can. Post scheduling can assist with this. Try to think about becoming an expert on your chosen subject matter. This is one way to gain a following.

5. Promote your blog. Use every social media you can possibly think of to advertise your blog posts. Of course, you don't want the conversations to always just be about you and your blog. You have to think creatively about the type of posts your readers will want to see and also interact on other's posts, too.

Book Reviewer

If you love to read, this may be a money-making opportunity for you. It will not bring you a full-time income, but it can allow you to have access to free books and earn a little money from home. A book review is an unbiased, honest assessment of a book. It can be as simple as giving a star rating to a multi-paragraph essay.

Because this book is about how to earn money from home, the only types of links offered for book review positions here are the ones that come with compensation. There are several more book review opportunities available, but their rewards are not monetary. They simply provide the glory of getting a free book or being able to publish your review on their site.

Kirkus Media:

https://www.kirkusreviews.com/about/careers/ The site itself does not mention how much it pays per review, but the book reviewer position is mentioned under the careers tab and is listed as a freelancer opportunity, indicating that there is some compensation involved. The site is looking for English and Spanish language reviewers for self-published authors. It states that anyone interested in the book reviewer position should submit their resume, writing sample, and a list of the reviewing specialties.

Reedsy Discovery:

https://reedsy.com/discovery/reviewers This site operates a little differently than other review sites. The compensation goes directly from readers to the reviewer in the form of a tip, with no structured or minimum amount.

Online Book Club:

https://onlinebookclub.org/free-books-for-reviews.php The book reviewer is offered a selection of books to review from, they choose the genre or book they prefer, and submit a review. The site lists the possible compensation to be $5-$60 per review. After you sign up, there is further fine print stating that you must adhere to strict review guidelines and that the first review you submit will not be for payment.

US Review of Books:
https://www.theusreview.com/USRreviewer.html# what Although the payment amount is not specified, the site does state that reviewers are paid monthly for reviews, and that checks are sent by the 5th of each month. The review itself only must be 250-300 words, but there are specific points to meet with each book review.

Chat Agents

What does a chat agent do? Chat agents communicate with customers through live chat or email to answer questions, solve problems, and troubleshoot. Chat agents can work remotely or in a standard office environment and are generally required to have customer service experience.

The chat agent position will require the candidate to have some level of customer involvement experience, typing skills, access to a computer, and the internet. Communication skills are crucial because that is the entire focus of the job. You will also need to be able to think quickly, multitask, carry on multiple conversations at once, problem-solve, and provide the physical equipment requirements.

Chat Shop:

https://jointhefamily.thechatshop.com/ The site states that they are only able to hire candidates from the UK and the US states of Florida, Georgia, Tennessee, and Texas. The Chat Shop's site states that "by blending Human Chat with AI Chat, we ensure that every conversation is focused on the visitors that need it most – on the conversations that matter." It does not specify the starting pay or exactly what equipment will be needed. It is assumed that you will at least need a computer with internet access and probably a good microphone and headset.

Kelly Connect:

https://www.kellyservices.us/us/other/kellyhome/ Kelly Connect Services requires their chat agents to have technical aptitude, customer service experience, communication skills, and a high school diploma or equivalent. In return, the site states that they are offering $13.50 per hour with a $1.00 increase after 90 days.

Smith.ai: https://smith.ai/careers This company has operating hours from 5am to 9pm PST, M-F, 6am to 4pm Saturday and Sunday and offers both part-time and full-time positions. For part-time, you must be available 5 days per week, 4 hours per day. The compensation was not mentioned, but it does state that you will need:

- Internet with less than 50 ms ping, greater than 10 Mbps download and 3Mbps upload.
- Typing skills of 40 wpm with 100% accuracy.

Sitestaff: https://www.sitestaffchat.com/chat-hosts/ Sitestaff is looking for sharp, experienced chat hosts with impeccable typing skills (65-75 wpm with perfect grammar, punctuation, and spelling), the ability to multitask, and strong empathy-driven communication skills. The site does not mention how much the starting pay will be.

Outplex: https://outplex.com/careers/ By their own definition, OutPLEX is "a top Teleservices contact center that supports recognized brands with Teleservices and Live Chat." The skills required are pretty basic. They require the ability to type 30-50wpm with outstanding spelling, grammar, and communication. The only physical equipment requirements listed are hardwired internet access and a non-MAC operating system with Windows access.

Customer Service Representative

An individual who serves as a customer service representative may be labeled under many different titles such as customer service representative, customer service advisor, customer service associate, or customer care agent. It could be any other combination of words that defines the job as one where an individual interacts with customers to answer questions, offer information, gather demographics, make suggestive sales, handle complaints, process orders, act as an ambassador to the company they are representing, and many other tasks and duties.

If you are a people person with good communication skills, typing skills, problem-solving skills, and the right home environment with the proper physical equipment, this may be a good job for you.

Most of these jobs will require some sort of home office that allows for a quiet workspace, varying types of equipment, and different levels of internet speed and software.

Because these jobs are structured much like an 'office' job or a 'call-center' job, they will offer and require structured schedules, set pay, and sometimes benefits.

Some of the entities hiring for some sort of customer involvement agent are:

Ttec: https://www.ttecjobs.com/en/work-from-home

American Express: https://jobs.americanexpress.com/jobs?keywords=virtual%20home%20based%20work%20from%20home&page=1

Broadpath: http://www.broad-path.com/join-our-team/careers/

Unum: https://unum.wd1.myworkdayjobs.com/External/1/refreshFacet/318c8bb6f553100021d223d9780d30be

Nexrep: https://nexrep.com/marketplace/

Sitel: https://jobs.sitel.com/job/Virtual-Work-from-Home-Inbound-Call-Center-Associate-Any/512652900/

The full list of companies hiring for customer service representatives, along with other pertinent available information, such as pay, qualifications, and equipment requirements, is in a different chapter of this book.

Closed Captioning

Closed captions are the words that you see at the bottom of the screen when you are watching a video, show, movie, or any other audiovisual file. The people who make these words grow from the spoken form into the written form are the captioners.

Usually, the process of creating closed captions is as follows. People are speaking (movie, show, lecture, etc.), a transcription is made where the spoken words are translated into a "script." Then the script is matched to the audiovisual so that the words being spoken go in time with the words being shown at the bottom of the screen. That is captioning.

There are two types of captioning: real-time and offline. Real-time captioning involves live programing. The captioner is creating the closed captions for all types of live programming, such as news broadcasts or sporting events.

Real-time captioning involves a great deal of speed and accuracy, and most captioning companies will require that you have the proper education, skills, and experience to work for them.

Offline captioning involves pre-recorded programming. The captioner will often create or use a script to match the words that are printed with the words that are spoken.

Real-time captioning:

Aberdeen: https://aberdeen.io/careers/ Candidates must have some experience, accuracy, and crazy speed: 180-220 wpm.

Offline captioning:

REV: https://www.rev.com/freelancers/captions This company offers captioning freelance work even to the inexperienced beginner. Beginner beware that even if you pass the test and can start with REV, it is very hard to make money that makes sense if you are not experienced. I was able to take the test in order to be qualified to get started, but then, when I took my first assignment, I realized how far out of my league I was.

Consulting

Are you already an expert at something? It doesn't matter what the field or specialty is, if you have a mountain of knowledge on any one subject matter or topic, then you are an expert and can be called on to be a consultant. Whether you are a licensed counselor, a beauty product guru, a knitting aficionado, kung fu master, dog groomer extraordinaire, or an HR bigwig with years of experience and knowledge, you are an expert on a specific field.

Use what you already have to your advantage and call yourself a consultant. This is the type of work from home opportunity that you would need to treat as your own business. You would want to define what your expertise is, where your skills are most marketable, who needs your help, and how to find them.

Once you have defined who you are and what you know, you can then broadcast your abilities to the world through a website, an online marketplace, a blog, social media, YouTube, and build a clientele. Again, being a consultant is generally a position where you would want to treat your expertise like the gold mine it is and create your own business rather than piecemeal your valuable time out.

You could also work for a new site that allows you to charge clients for consulting services on an hourly basis. **Grinfer** https://grinfer.com/ allows you to sign up as a consultant offering your expertise to whoever is willing to pay for your time. You can also easily publish courses that will further brand yourself as an expert in your field.

Data Entry

A data entry clerk is a member of staff employed to enter or update data into a computer system. Most of these positions are considered entry-level and are offered pay commensurate with an entry-level position. The basic requirements will be to have some reading, writing, and typing skills.

Axion Data Entry Services:
https://axiondata.com/employment/ Requires 2-3 years of data entry experience and a keystroke rate of 15,000 keystrokes per hour. The site states that it offers long term independent contractor positions on a rare basis that a position comes available and to weed out the unqualified candidates. There is a fee to register with their database of $5, $7, or $10, depending on how long you want your information to be retained.

SigTrack: https://sigtrack.net/ While this company is not currently hiring, it is one of the few that actually hires for data entry positions solely, specifically to link grassroots campaigns with data entry freelancers to update the information obtained from voter registration and petitions.

Editing and Proofreading

The Merriam Webster dictionary has three definitions for the word edit. Of the three definitions, each starts with two words: to prepare, to assemble, and to alter. So, an editor prepares a text for publication by assembling words that have been written and then altered. Proofreading is "the reading of a galley proof or an electronic copy of a publication to find and correct production errors."

What's the difference between proofreading and editing? Proofreading focuses on stylistic errors in writing, such as grammar, punctuation, spelling, and syntax. Editing includes all of the steps in proofreading while also making changes to a written work of art or communication to make it easier to understand.

Cactus Communications:

https://www.cactusglobal.com/careers/work-from-home#wfh This site is best for editors with a bachelor's degree or higher with a science, humanities, or engineering background. You don't have to have editing experience, just the proper education.

Edit 911: https://edit911.com/employment/ Applicants must have a Ph.D. in English or another discipline that is writing intensive.

Enago: https://www.enago.com/careers/current-openings.htm Extensive experience and education required to apply for positions on this site.

Gramlee: https://www.gramlee.com/jobs.html The site states that they are always looking for exceptional editors.

Lifetips: https://www.lifetips.com/about/join-team-editorial.html Simple application process for editors with search engine marketing experience and knowledge.

American Journal Experts: https://rscontractors.applytojob.com/apply This is an academic site hiring for professional editors who have scholarly knowledge on topics such as math, science, medicine, and physics.

E-Commerce

E-commerce is the activity of electronically buying or selling products or services online. This type of money-making opportunity has so many different avenues, offshoots, and side notes that it is really a book of its own. Here, I will go over the basic core of types of e-commerce, and then the rest is up to you.

Remember that e-commerce should be treated more like operating a business that is yours and, as such, should be treated with the same amount of deference. Practice due diligence. Conduct thorough research and make sure that this an avenue you are sure to want to delve into before diving in headfirst.

There are 6 basic types of e-commerce: business to business, business to consumer, consumer to consumer, consumer to business, business to administration, and consumer to administration.

- Business to business (B2B) e-commerce involves the electronic transaction of goods and sales conducted between two companies. For example, a motorcycle repair shop may purchase repair supplies from a motorcycle supply chain via an online transaction.

- Business to consumer (B2C) e-commerce is the same as above, but the transaction is from a business to a consumer. For example, anytime you order something from Amazon, the business, it has conducted an e-commerce transaction with you, the consumer.

- Consumer to consumer (C2C) e-commerce involves an online transaction between two consumers. The eBay platform would be a good example of two consumers enacting a C2C e-commerce transaction.

- Consumer to business (C2B) takes place anytime a consumer offers a product or service to a business, and an electronic exchange takes place. For example, a product reviewer is paid to test a product and issue its findings for said business.

- Business to administration (B2A) refers to e-commerce taking place between a business and a public administrative entity. For example, anytime a business has to register with a federal or state entity to process their employees' taxes.

- Consumer to administration (C2A) is the process of e-commerce involving a consumer and a public administrative organization. For example, when an individual files their individual taxes with the IRS.

Ways that you can work in the e-commerce field include:

- Amazon FBA, which we will examine in-depth in a later chapter.

- Running an eBay store
- Running an Etsy store
- Offering online accounting and tax filing services
- Run your own website selling items of your choice
- Start a t-shirt printing and merchandise store on Spreadshirt.com

Email Support

Email support is a form of communication that allows for a customer and business representative to communicate in order to resolve customer questions, challenges, and concerns without both parties having to be present for the conversation at the same time. For people who excel in customer service but don't want to or can't be on the phone, this is another alternative to put these skills to use. Customer service-oriented jobs that require speaking to customers on the phone also tend to have stricter and more extensive physical equipment requirements. Email support is not done live, so the equipment standards tend to be a bit easier.

ModSquad:

https://jobs.lever.co/modsquad/e3f780a3-1610-4244-b370-57ba181699ef The title of the role they are hiring for is a community support associate, but this job's duties entail customer interactions via email, so it located here in email support. This company is looking for individuals with extensive written communication skills, technical knowledge and aptitude, customer service experience, and preferably with knowledge and passion for live video streaming. The position is listed as full-time, with competitive salary and benefits. There are no equipment qualifications listed, only states that security software will need to be installed by ModSquad.

Ynab: https://ynab.recruiterbox.com/jobs/fk0qmra/ This is a combination role of email support and chat. Ynab is looking for part-time support specialists who can commit to 25-30 hours per week, are flawless communicators who can easily handle several conversations at once, and are genuinely customer service oriented. The listed pay is $18 per hour during training, with an increase to $20 per hour for permanent part-time. To apply, visit the link and follow the instructions to submit a cover letter, answer the questions listed, and submit a resume.

Whoop: https://www.whoop.com/careers/ The positions that Whoop is currently hiring for are for membership services representative for second and third shift, 3pm-1130pm or 11pm-730am. It is a multifaceted role addressing and serving customers through email, phone, and chat. The required qualifications all focus on customer service skills such as troubleshooting, written and oral communication skills, being reliable and punctual, and the ability to stay calm and professional. There are a few listed physical requirements, such as having a quiet, distraction-free workspace, internet of 25 Mbps download, and 5 Mbps upload. Whoop provides all the needed equipment. The starting pay is $18.00 per hour with benefits and paid time off. Unfortunately, this position is only available in about half of the states. See the site for a full listing as the offered locations are dynamic.

Moderator

In the online sense, a moderator promotes interactions in forums, answers questions as they arise, updates the website, or blog with questions from participants and members. The moderator may also monitor the company or website's social media accounts such as Facebook and Twitter to react and respond to comments, posts, message boards, and chats. This position is complimentary to a social media manager, as some of the tasks may overlap.

Liveworld: https://www.liveworld.com/HR/US/
This company calls its moderator position a "social media customer care agent." In this role, the qualified applicant will monitor social media posts, take appropriate action, respond to customer's questions and comments, and keep apprised of emerging trends and topics. The experience that is required is a customer service background, dependable internet, a laptop, and the post mentions being fluent in languages other than English.

The Social Element: https://thesocialelement.agency/jobs/ With this organization, the position is titled "community manager," and its post states that internally, the role is referred to as an "engagement specialist." They are seeking an individual with a strong social media background, experience with all the platforms, and a flexible schedule. Visit the link with your updated resume and with the answers to the posted questions to inquire about the opportunity.

Music

If you're a musician and are good at what you do, you can find many ways to make a living by practicing your trade. You may not land the next big record deal, but you certainly use your talent to your advantage. Here are some general suggestions on how to make money with music.

- Create a true fan base and hold onto them. These are the people that will follow you wherever you go, buy all your music and your merchandise. Find a target audience and make sure that your music marketing strategy is focused on them.

- Direct your traffic. Wherever your social media is, make sure that there is an easy link directing people to your music sites as well, that way, you lose no potential fans.

- Advertising is still important. Just because you have the voice of an angel doesn't mean its magically being heard amidst all the internet noise. Advertise and bring them to you.

- Pre-orders are crucial. Create and maintain a much larger footprint by focusing on brand awareness, preparation, and branding.

- Crowdfunding cannot be forgotten. You need funds to keep going. Try checking out a crowdfunding site and model what the most successful artists have done.

- MP3 sales are still a good source of sales.

- Don't forget CDs. Some fans will still want that hard copy after the show.

- Merchandise from your brand gives fans a piece of you to keep with them, monopolize on it.

Some platforms where musicians can earn real money for what they do include: Soundcloud, YouTube, and TuneCore. You could also consider setting up a room in your house as a recording studio. You could not only record your own hits and produce an album, but you could rent the space to other musicians in need of recording.

You could also become a composer for video games or write background music for video creators. YouTubers need unique music, and you could license your creations to them for use on their channel. Independent video game companies are always in need of original scores for their video games, too. These could be recorded at home on your computer and transacted online.

If you're good at writing jingles, partner with a local marketing company or advertising production studio. You could also find community groups that perform for special events or bars and restaurants to partner with. While this option isn't exactly working "from home," it is on your own schedule and on your own terms.

Online Poker

Playing poker online for grins and giggles is completely acceptable and legal in all 50 states. Playing poker online for money is another matter. It is technically gambling, which is technically illegal in most places. For now, it is only legal in Delaware, New Jersey, Nevada, and Pennsylvania. So, for those who want to try their skill and luck playing poker to make money, you will need to go to an offshore poker site to keep it legal.

Check out these offshore poker sites if poker is your thing and you want to make, or lose, some cash:

Ignition Casino:
https://www.ignitioncasino.eu/betting-offers/poker-welcome-bonus?referral=0Qo-EFPzOnss-htah9CPemNd7ZgqdRLk&affid=11851

BET online: https://promotions.betonline.ag/100-poker-special-bonus?btag=E5MH4-jgmgxuQfriZQUYE2Nd7ZgqdRLk&affid=82486

Intertops Poker: https://poker.intertops.eu/en/

Juicy Stakes: https://www.juicystakes.eu/register

Americas Cardroom:
https://www.americascardroom.eu/

Podcasts

It is possible to make money with a successful podcast. It will take time, effort, dedication, discipline, strategy, and a certain amount of investment. This is not an opportunity to make a quick buck or an immediate paycheck. Rather, this is a work from home opportunity that should be treated more as your own business where you would see results later down the road.

This is another route to establishing yourself as an expert on a topic or as someone that people look to for a certain niche. Consider crafting your podcast around a single area of expertise. A podcast, a blog, social media, and a YouTube channel can all work collectively in creating a brand experience that makes you real money.

This approach is similar to the blogger or YouTuber job in that there are some common paths to monetizing a podcast:

Affiliate Marketing: Recommend products and services to your audience that they will like. The podcaster earns income from this route by earning a commission from the product or service provider whose goods they recommended and sold.

Sponsorship: After there is some success with the affiliate marketing, then you will be able to enlist sponsors to help fund your podcast.

Coaching: Once you have an audience who knows you, trusts you, and recommends you, then you can sell your coaching services. See "consulting" that we covered earlier in this book.

Courses/Lessons: Over time, you will start to identify the recurring questions that need to be addressed in the coaching sessions. These questions can be turned into a course. Your knowledge can turn into dollars. You could sell these courses online for more profit. Try sites like Skillshare, Grinfer, and Udemy.

Product Sales: Lastly, build a product or service that helps your students/audience solve the problems that brought them to your podcast for your assistance.

Merchandise Sales: Consider selling t-shirts, mugs, tote bags, and mouse pads with something related to your brand like your catchphrase, logo, or an "inside joke" created while interacting with your audience that your loyal followers will understand.

Programming

Since computer programming is a series of work tasks that are pretty much always done on a computer, online, then it is one of the ideal jobs to do from home. You will need a certain technical aptitude and a level of education to be able to land a job like this.

Some of the job titles included in computer programming include:

- Software application developer
- Web developer
- Computer systems engineer
- Database administrator
- Computer systems analyst
- Software quality assurance engineer
- Business intelligence analyst
- Computer programmer
- Network system administrator

These are high paying opportunities for those individuals who have the right skill set and education to be able to perform the job duties.

Check out some of these tech companies for great work from home opportunities utilizing all that techie wisdom:

https://www.grammatech.com/careers

https://fisicoinc.com/careers

https://www.ntiva.com/careers

https://www.datavail.com/about/careers/

https://www.lockheedmartinjobs.com/career-areas

The list can go on and on for pages and pages.

Realistically, if you already have the education and skills required for these types of jobs, then you probably already know where and how to find the job. For those individuals who are very tech minded and are thinking of making a move towards education, remember that there are literally thousands of these jobs for the people who are properly qualified.

Once you have the knowledge and skills, you are remotely employable for life, which is definitely a plus considering that our entire world is becoming more and more tech-centered every day. Job security is crucial, and you won't find a job much more secure than these.

Telemedicine

All areas of our lives are being influenced and driven by technology, even medicine. The influx of telecommunication and constantly evolving technology has allowed more medical professionals to be able to work remotely. Where medical practitioners and patients once had to meet face to face for every issue, there is now a new practice in place – telemedicine.

Telemedicine allows healthcare workers to meet with patients remotely, discuss symptoms, medical issues, receive a diagnosis, learn treatment options, and more. Obviously, you must have the necessary education and experience to practice medicine to be able to perform this sort of job. On that note, these companies also employ technical workers to keep their platform running smoothly, insurance adjusters, and sometimes intake specialists, appointment setters, customer service reps, and medical billing experts, and transcriptionists.

American Well: https://providers.amwell.com/

MD Live: https://www.mdlive.com/careers/

Doctor on Demand:
https://www.doctorondemand.com/about-us/careers

Axispoint Health: https://careers-axispointhealth.icims.com/

Steady MD: https://www.steadymd.com/careers/

Research and Fact-Checking

An online researcher is someone who is able to conduct research on the internet to compile and analyze data from a multitude of sources to present to their client in a way that is easy to understand. A good researcher is one that can dig beneath the surface to find the facts from credible sources with accurate information by asking good questions, having lots of patience and a general love of knowledge. Most online research work is done on a freelance or contract basis.

Upwork, one of the online marketplaces to find freelance work, has a lot of postings for internet researchers.

Additionally, here are some companies who are also looking for researchers:

Wonder Research:

https://start.askwonder.com/researcher/application/start Looking for applicants with strong research skills, preferably a bachelor's degree or higher, and pays $15-18 per hour.

BBE Marketing:

https://bbemarketing.com/careers/ This company titles their research role, 'research engineer,' and the individual for this position would be researching and verifying data and interacting with partners and team members.

Nox Solutions:

https://www.noxsolutions.com/join-our-team The researcher position here is a full-time, remote position with 401k and benefits. Nox is looking for someone with research skills and preferably a degree in business administration with a legal company background.

Resume Writer

Having a proper resume that highlights who you are and what your most valuable skills and qualities are can make the difference in whether you get the job you deserve. For anyone who struggles with creating that perfect resume, there are resume writing services available. A resume writer will be the one who translates your awesomeness into the written word for the ideal employment.

Talent Inc: https://www.talentinc.com/remote-careers/ This company seeks writers with at least 3 years of professional experience who are Microsoft Office geniuses. The site states that there is enough work to keep you busy, making up to $3,500 per month.

Resume Writers:
https://www.resumewriters.com/

The Job Sauce: https://thejobsauce.com/career/ This contract position is only for the most qualified resume writer. The Job Sauce is looking for people with 5 or more years of experience writing resumes, having edited a minimum of 75 resumes with a list of other required qualifications. The contractor is paid per resume on a weekly basis.

Reviewer

Yes, people really get paid to review books, products, services, and websites. No, it is not fraudulent if you are giving an accurate, honest review of the book, product, service, or website. The people who are paid to give these reviews are being compensated for their time with the expectation that they are being honest and factual.

While there are plenty of companies out there that pay for fraudulent, high rating reviews in order to boost their online presence, there are also others that will pay you with either cash, gift cards, or a product. If you are a blogger, a social media influencer, or a YouTube star, then you have access to many more paid review opportunities.

For everyone else who stays under the radar and just wants to make a couple dollars or get some free products, check out this list:

User Testing: https://www.usertesting.com/be-a-user-tester#collapse1 This site pays $10 via PayPal for every twenty-minute video you complete seven days after the test is completed. Basically, you download the user testing software, complete a series of tasks while speaking your thoughts out loud, and you are sent the ten bucks a week later.

Pro Chef Kitchen Tools:
https://prochefkitchentools.com/pages/pr#gs.4lf5y
e Sign up for their ambassador program. Pick a product, then test and use the product. Write a review. Keep the product. That seems to be the program in a nutshell.

GMYLE: https://www.gmyle.com/collection/lab
Purchase the product. Provide proof of the purchase. Get reimbursed. Test and review the product. Each user allowed up to 2 samples per month. Seems pretty straightforward.

Search Engine Evaluator

A search engine evaluator is a person who is hired by companies who need humans to verify search results. This individual helps to ensure that internet searches are returning relevant, accurate, comprehensive results from the searches performed on search engines.

Most of these positions are contract or freelance. Most companies are looking for people who have a degree. Most of the hiring entities prefer that the candidate be bilingual and at least proficient in English.

Appen: https://connect.appen.com/qrp/public/jobs Appen regularly employs freelancers to work four to five hours per weekday, performing a variety of search engine tasks. They are hired after passing a series of exams.

Lionbridge: https://www.lionbridge.com/join-our-team/ Similar to Appen, Lionbridge also seeks freelancers to perform search engine evaluations.

Social Media Influencer

Are you a social media fanatic? Do you spend lots of time checking your social media and connecting with others on their social media? Well, maybe consider growing that passion for social media interaction into a way to make some extra money or turn into a career.

Similar to blogging or podcasts, there are a few ways to turn your followers and all those hours you spend on social media into a profit. The only thing to keep in mind is that it will need to be treated like a business, and there will need to be investments made in with time, money, and effort.

Basically, you can use whatever platform(s) you choose to:

- Build a follower base and network
- Use the platform to publish ads for monetization
- Find a niche and become an expert on a topic
- Use that expertise to coach others on the subject matter
- Take that coaching experience and create a course that can be marketed and sold

It is not easy. You have to build a following, develop expertise, invest time and money, not give up, and be in it for the long haul. Do your research and know what the reality of what you are trying to do before thinking you will be the next overnight YouTube star making a million a year.

Another spin on the idea of a social media influencer is a social media manager. This position would basically monitor and run social media accounts for a business. You would need to know the latest trends, how to make the most of hashtags, and what the intended customer/audience of the business is interested in. You would be expected to run the social media account, so the business can gain followers who turn into customers while also appeasing current customers.

Social media manager jobs that can be done remotely are usually found on job websites like Indeed and Glassdoor. Some really good training for social media managers would be the Google AdWords certification training (free from Google) or obtaining a certificate in social media management from an online training school such as Udemy.

Teaching

Among the helping professions, teachers may be the most vital to our society, and, unfortunately, some of the most underappreciated and undervalued. If you have a degree, certification, or a set of skills or knowledge with which to share with the world, please do so. We all need you.

Udemy:

https://www.udemy.com/teaching/?ref=teach_head er If you have a set of skills or a knowledge bank that others might find useful, turn it into a course, and earn money on Udemy every time a student purchases your course.

VIPKid:

https://www.vipkid.com/mkt/faq/becoming-teacher
An online classroom that teaches English to kids in China.
You must have a bachelor's degree and then go through an
application process. You create a profile, acquire some
students, and get paid to teach remotely.

Preply: https://preply.com/en/skype/tutoring-
jobs Preply is an online turning platform for tutors and
students to connect so that students can work on their skills
in different languages and subjects.

IXL Learning:

https://www.ixl.com/company/careers IXL is a home-
based learning site and has openings for math content
writer, math copy editor, Spanish translator, and the hiring
positions change upon need.

Test Graders

Test graders are also called readers/evaluators, and their
job is to score the student responses on exams. The exams
may cover such subjects such as language arts, math, science,
or a range of other topics. They are usually hired on a

contract, temporary basis during certain peak times of the year.

Measurement Inc.:

https://www.measurementinc.com/careers/reader-evaluator-job-description You will need to have a bachelor's degree in any field with a successful interview, and most of the jobs are available March to June.

Write Score:

https://www.writescore.com/become-a-scorer/ With Write Score, you will only have to have a two-year degree, but you will need to pass a qualifying test, then go through orientation, pass qualification levels, and then finally begin scoring student responses. The first orientation starts in late July to early August.

Literably: https://literably.com/scorer-signup No degree needed, just the ability to pass the qualification testing. Literably is an online platform to help test students reading levels through oral testing. They do not hire anyone from the states of CA, CT, MA, MT, NE, or NJ.

Transcription

If you are a talented typist, you may want to look into transcription work. A transcriptionist is a person who takes audio files, handwritten documents, or other communications and converts them into text format by typing in what they hear or see.

Because the process of converting the spoken word into text goes extremely fast, most transcriptionists go through training and utilize the help of a foot pedal so that they can type and review the audio file at the same time.

Speakwrite:

https://speakwrite.com/transcription-jobs/transcriptionist-application-steps/ There is a 5-step process to being hired on to work transcription jobs with Speakwrite. You will have to apply, pass a typing test, sign a confidentiality agreement and provide work history, go through training and over the company policies, and then start taking training jobs before you start taking paid jobs.

GMR Transcription:

https://www.gmrtranscription.com/careers-for-apply_general_transcriptionist.aspx This company has a basic online application. After submission, you will then receive an email with a link and instructions to a test, and then you go from there.

Daily Transcription:

https://www.dailytranscription.com/careers/ Daily Transcription's site states that they offer a higher compensation rate than some of their other competitors, along with a comprehensive training program for the newbie transcriptionists. Their application process for this 1099 position includes a skills assessment test and a transcription test. They highly recommend the use of transcription software, good headphones, and a foot pedal.

Speechpad:

https://www.speechpad.com/worker/jobs/transcribers The 1099 position is like the other transcription positions listed with slightly lower pay rates. The site states that the pay ranges from .25-1.00 per minute. They pay through PayPal every Tuesday and Friday.

Go Transcript:

https://gotranscript.com/transcription-jobs Always hiring, the site states that they pay up to .60 per minute, with average earnings per month of $150, and top monthly pay of $1,215.

Translation

An online translator takes written or spoken material from one language and uses their competent grasp of both languages to translate it into another language. These individuals are in high demand as people from all over the globe can interact over the internet and need to be able to communicate clearly, despite any language or dialect barriers.

Cyracom: http://careers.cyracom.com/ic A successful candidate must have an interpretation degree. Looking for people who speak two or more languages to be phone interpreters.

Gengo: https://gengo.com/translators/ A Lionbridge company, the translator position is paid twice monthly. The site asks you to sign up before offering any specific information, such as pay or requirements.

Interpreters and Translators: https://www.ititranslates.com/who-we-are/join-our-team-2/ Always looking for professional interpreters and translators with strong language skills in two or more languages. The successful candidate will pass an oral exam and a background check with a preference for people with medical or legal specialization.

Certified Languages International:

https://certifiedlanguages.com/careers/ As their language needs fluctuate constantly, Certified Languages International is always looking for highly qualified candidates with court interpreter certification programs such as CCHI, NBCMI, DHS, and others.

Language Line Solutions:

https://www.languageline.com/careers Qualified applicants will speak English and one or more other languages with a high degree of fluency, have some computer skills, and an exceptional customer service sense.

Travel Agent

A good travel agent will be able to help you discover whatever part of the world you are wanting to explore. A travel agent's role is to assist the traveler in planning their trip. They help to arrange transportation, lodging, admission to entertainment activities for individuals and groups, make suggestions for dining, and overall ensure that the traveler's trip is smooth and successful.

There are two types of travel agent jobs. One type is where you work from home and create your own franchise, and the pay is all commission. The other is a more traditional work from home role where you work remotely for a company, earning a base pay plus commission, sometimes with benefits.

Air Treks: https://www.airtreks.com/about/jobs-at-airtreks/

BCD Travel: https://www.bcdtravel.com/careers/

CCRA Travel Commerce Network: https://www.ccra.com/jobs/

Kemp Travel Group: https://kemptravel.com/careers/

Video Editor

A video editor is involved in video production and the post-production of film making. The video editor's responsibilities involve decisions about the selection and combing of shots into sequences, as well as the addition of accompanying sound effects and music to ultimately create a finished movie, television program, commercial, promo, or snipe.

A video editor needs to have media production, computer operating soft and hardware knowledge and needs to have sharp attention to detail. Online video consumption continues to climb every year in giant leaps and bounds. That means that a job or career path in video editing can be financially solvent and stable.

Many of the remote video editing jobs and gigs I found were located on Upwork, an online marketplace for freelancers. Upwork had opportunities for all skill levels, from the beginner to the highest qualified professional.

Because videos are used so widely for marketing, sales, demonstration, interaction, and so many other functions, the jobs available for video editing are for a variety of industries and types of companies.

The list below is just a sample of the companies that are hiring now for video editing.

Manning Publications:

https://www.manning.com/careers Looking for a developmental video editor to work with video course instructors to create and edit high-quality courses.

DoSayGive: https://dosaygive.com/dosaygive-is-hiring-2020/ Hiring for a full-time creative assistant whose duties include video editing with exquisite taste in fashion, interior, and lifestyle.

JOMI: https://jomi.com/careers The Journal of Medical Insight is looking for video production staff to film and edit surgical film.

By the time that this text is released, some of these job opportunities may have been filled. There is always freelance work from home gigs on Upwork and other online job marketplaces.

Video editing is a highly sought-after skill and can bring someone a fair and reliable source of income.

Virtual Assistant

A virtual assistant is someone who provides administrative services such as customer service, data entry, emailing, scheduling, and various other tasks to clients outside of the client's office. Some skills and qualifications that are necessary for a successful virtual assistant are exceptional customer service, computer, administrative, internet usage, and marketing.

Online job marketplaces such as Upwork and Zirtual regularly have these types of positions open, with a variety of freelance and contract terms. Some of the opportunities may be limited to a few days, a single set of tasks, or be longer-term with more commitment from both parties.

Fancy Hands: https://www.fancyhands.com/jobs This platform only hires virtual assistants. Their website states that they have assistants located all over the world to help alleviate the workload by taking over tasks such as calling, scheduling, data entry, research, purchase, and concierge services.

Use these online marketplaces to search for virtual assistant positions:

- Zirtual https://www.zirtual.com/

- UpWork https://www.upwork.com/
- Remote.co https://remote.co/
- Homejobstaffing
  https://homejobstaffing.com/
- LinkedIn https://www.linkedin.com/
- Indeed https://www.indeed.com/
- ZipRecruiter https://www.ziprecruiter.com/
- Craigslist

Voice Services

Another way to earn money from home is to do voice-overs. A voice-over is read from a script and may be spoken by someone who appears elsewhere in the production or by a specialist voice talent. You could be that voice talent!

These sites will pay you to use your voice:

Filmless:
https://www.smartrecruiters.com/Filmless/829035 80-freelance-voice-over-artist This organization is hiring for highly experienced individuals with over five years of voice over experience. Must have a portfolio showcasing

their work and a studio at home with which to perform the work.

Snap Recordings:

https://www.snaprecordings.com/become-a-voice-talent There is no information offered to specify the type of person, skills, equipment, or qualifications necessary for this position, just a form of interest to fill out and send in.

Voices.com: https://www.voices.com/ This site is an online job marketplace used solely for professional voice actors.

Voice 123: https://voice123.com/plans Another online marketplace for voice actors. There are various plans available for sign up.

Voice Crafters:

https://www.voicecrafters.com/log-in-join/?redirect=dashboard#talent_submission_section Only the most experienced voice over actors are accepted on this site. They are looking for individuals with over five years of experience and an at-home studio.

Website and App Testing

The creators of websites and apps must know how it is going to function when it is being used in the real world. So, they offer users the opportunity to try out their websites and apps with some sort of compensation for their time.

While it is not something you can turn into a full-time income, it will help you to earn some extra money, and it is something you can do on your own time, at your own pace, with a minimum of equipment. Because each site has a limited amount of pay offered and limited opportunities, it helps to sign up with as many sites as possible.

User Testing: https://www.usertesting.com/be-a-user-tester This site requires that you visit websites or use apps, speaking aloud as you complete tasks to create a 20-minute video, and you are paid $10 via PayPal seven days later.

U Test: https://www.utest.com/ At U Test, users are asked to "read articles, rate tools, learn new skills, find paid projects, and chat about tech, careers, and trends."

What Users Do:

http://panel.whatusersdo.com/become-a-tester/
Here, users are paid $5 for each task successfully completed via PayPal on the 25th of each month.

Enroll: https://enrollapp.com/ The tests and tasks administered through this site are easier to perform and complete, but that does mean it comes with a much smaller payout.

User Feel: https://www.userfeel.com/ You'll be paid $10 for each test you take, and each test takes about 10-20 minutes each.

TryMyUI:

https://www.trymyui.com/worker/signup This site also pays $10 for a test that lasts about 20 minutes. They are looking for a video featuring you using the app or website along with a written response.

Userlytics: https://www.userlytics.com/tester-signup The Userlytics platform offers a three-step process: a) register, b) interact with the web or a mobile app, c) get paid by PayPal. Compensation offered per test is quoted as being five to twenty dollars with as much as $90 being the payout for some projects.

Testing Time: https://www.testingtime.com/en/become-a-paid-testuser/ Claims that you can make up to $50 per hour taking tests that you qualify for.

Intellizoom: https://www.intellizoom.com/ The standard survey pays an average of $2. For the surveys that require you to think out loud on audio and video, you will be paid $10. These payments are made 21 days after the results are approved. The results typically take 3-5 days to get approved.

Validately: https://panel.validately.com/signup This site offers talk aloud tests that pay $5-10 per test, each test takes about 5 minutes. The moderated live tests that are offered require a webcam and pay $25 for 30 minutes.

Ubertester: https://ubertesters.com/become-tester/ The pay is not mentioned at the beginning of the sign-up process; it does state that some previous experience may be required.

Loop11: https://www.loop11.com/get-paid-to-test-websites/ You will need to have a microphone and webcam to be eligible for Loop11. The site has you do a short qualification test before being able to sign up.

UserBrain: https://tester.userbrain.net/ This site pays a little less, $3 for each approved test video. Each test video should be able 5-15 minutes to complete, it gets approved, and then you get paid via PayPal.

Testbirds: https://nest.testbirds.com/home/tester No payout information is available at the beginning of the signup process. It is similarly structured to other website/app testing sites.

Writing

If communication via the written word is your forte, check out some of the sites below. The writing sites that don't require a lot of experience are good for beginners also offer beginners pay too, sometimes offering as little as less than two cents per word.

Just like every other industry, the higher educated and the more technically skilled you are, the higher your pay and perks.

A pass education:

https://apasseducation.com/job-openings/ This site is seeking highly-skilled, academic, professional academic writers with degrees and topic-specific education and experience.

A list apart:

https://alistapart.com/about/contribute/ A list apart hires writers with enough technical skill and knowledge to write for an audience of designers, developers, content strategists, and information architects. Be prepared to go through an intense, extensive screening process.

Back to college:

http://www.back2college.com/guide.htm Pays $55 for 1,000 to 1500 words 30 days after publication by PayPal or check. Topics are related to nontraditional students (over 30 years old) returning to school.

Bestpickist: https://bestpickist.com/write-for-us/
Writers needed to provide informational content and reviews.

BKA Content:
https://www.bkacontent.com/write-for-bka/ This opportunity is best for SEO content writers, product description writers, and legal content writers. Pay is $1.35 to 5 cents per word depending on skill level and is paid every two weeks via PayPal.

Clearvoice: https://clearvoice.com/signup You will need to create a profile and then get matched to work, and the pay is ten cents per word.

Contentdivas: https://contentdivas.com/write-for-content-divas/ Writers should be skilled in content and research writing. The site is looking for writers who want to write on a consistent basis.

Content Remarketing:
http://www.contentremarketing.com/write-for-us/
Content Remarketing prefers experienced, strong writers with specialties and expertise on specific subject matters.

Content Runner:

https://www.contentrunner.com/ This site matches writers with content seekers for a variety of topics.

Getabstract:

https://www.getabstract.com/en/writers/applicatio n To get more information, you read an article and submit a short summary along with your contact information. The site states that upon receipt of your submission, you will be contacted within 10 days. If you are a successful candidate, you will have access to open freelancer assignments.

YouTube Content Creator

There are plenty of folks who want to become an overnight YouTube star and be launched into instant riches and fame. It's quite a bit harder than that and involves way more work than people realize.

The following information comes straight from YouTube, detailing how you can build a YouTube channel and work on creating a revenue you can earn from home. The YouTube Creator Academy narrows it down to three steps:

1. Building an engaged audience. Your content can be amazing, but you have to have people watching it in order to begin to think about monetizing your channel. So, make sure that you are connecting and creating a community of people who tune in to your channel to bring your numbers to where they need to be. Subscription count, view time minutes, and engagements like comments and likes/dislikes make or break your channel.

2. Join the YouTube Partner Program. After your channel has been up for 12 months, has 1,000 subscribers, and 4,000 watch hours, you become eligible to monetize your channel by being able to have ads run on your videos.

3. Make money with ads and other options. Ads are the most significant source of revenue from a successful YouTube channel.

Be sure to create engaging content that stays advertiser-friendly because some advertisers will be using targeting tools to reach certain target demographics. You should consider making your channel about one genre or one specialty thing. You really should not mix different categories of videos on one channel. For instance, if you're an ASMR channel, your audience may not necessarily be interested in you also playing Minecraft or posting a vlog of your vacation time.

Other sources of income from a YouTube channel can be from:

- channel memberships
- merchandise sales
- super chat donations
- brand deals
- affiliate marketing partnerships
- YouTube premium

It is possible to create a source of income from a successful YouTube channel. That does not mean that it is easy. It will take investments in time doing research, time creating content, money to get the proper recording gear, effort in making videos, and there will be plenty of challenges along the way. This work from home opportunity is like a startup business and should be viewed as such and treated that way.

You will need to heavily research marketing strategies such as selecting the proper keywords, hashtags, video descriptions, and titles to make your video be picked up by the YouTube algorithm. Learning how to create an effective thumbnail is just like creating a cover for a book; most people will judge your content off of that first 2-second cursory glance as they are scrolling through their suggested videos feed.

There are entire volumes of books dedicated to running and growing a successful YouTube channel. In this book, since the topic is not solely dedicated to this particular work from home job, I would encourage you to do more research if this is a job that interests you.

Additionally, a content creator is not just expected to be proficient in managing their videos and channel; they must also be excellent at mastering social media. You will find that most successful content creators also manage a Twitter, Facebook Page, and Instagram related to their channel brand. This can also branch out into podcasting, blogging, and even writing an eBook – all in the name of your YouTube brand.

This job is much more about marketing, brand management, and social media than it is about producing video content. Yes, your videos need to be entertaining, informative, and/or engaging, but you also need to truly connect to your audience (aka your "customer.") Again, there are many texts about how to do this effectively.

Chapter 6: 64 Specific Companies Hiring Remote Workers

The listings below were compiled through Internet searches, search engine queries, from inside information from Facebook groups I joined, and from lists from bloggers on where to find legitimate work from home opportunities.

Some of the remote positions are of the traditional type, a paycheck, and a schedule, you're just doing it from home.

Some are freelancer opportunities where you are an independent contractor, paid without taxes being taken out, and you are in complete control of your own timing. Others are a combination of both. The entire list is in alphabetical order.

These jobs are from real companies that hire for a range of job titles. Most of these jobs are some sort of customer service in orientation, will have some requirements as far as what type of hardware and internet you will need to have and often have a waitlist. Additionally, most of these jobs will require experience, clean background, and, oftentimes, an extensive interview process.

In this list, there are positions open for people with little to no experience all the way to the highly technical, skilled, and experience. Try to apply to as many companies as possible. Positions come and go quickly. Cast a wide net and apply to several or many of the companies listed and take the offer that is most appealing to you. The wait can be worth it when you're sitting at home, working around your own schedule, and living your best life.

Please note that not every job is available in every state. Pay attention to geographical location requirements.

Companies have reasons for establishing why they can only operate in certain locales. If not stated, then the position either did not indicate a geographical requirement, or it was available anywhere.

Accolade Support:

https://www.accoladesupport.com/agents-application-out.html Accolade Support is a US-based call center and marketing service that provides call center services for numerous other companies and organizations.

Equipment you will need:

- Telephone with a headset
- PC with Windows 7 or better
- Hard-wired high-speed internet
- Quiet work environment

You must be able to work 25 hours or more per week. The physical requirements are much simpler for this role. You just have to have internet access, a computer, and a phone to be able to make calls.

Activus Connect:

https://activusconnect.com/join-our-team/ Activus

connect is a Customer Experience Provider (CXP) of outsourced solutions for brands who understand the value of authentic, human conversations. Their "Ambassador – Processing Support" position is assisting unemployment applicants with the unemployment application process. The ideal candidate will have over ten years of experience in a service industry craft with strong communication and customer service skills.

The physical equipment requirements:

- Desktop or laptop (no Macs)
- Windows 7 or newer
- 2 GHz or better
- Ram: 4gb or better
- Hard drive: 20gb or better
- All peripherals must be wired.
- Hard wired, high-speed internet with 10MB download, 3MB upload
- Noise-canceling headset and microphone
- Webcam
- A second monitor is highly recommended

Pay is $15 per hour.

Advanis: https://www.advanis.net/careers Advanis is a market and policy research company that has been doing surveys since 1997, and we are looking for telephone interviewers. Currently, they offer a "Telephone Research Interviewer" position with working hours of Monday through Friday 3-10pm (MST) and Saturdays 10am to 5pm (MST). You need moderate typing skills (30 wpm), customer service skills, and the ability to work the hours listed.

Equipment requirements:

- High-speed internet
- Phone line (landline) in the home office space
- Corded headset with noise-canceling microphone
- Computer (MAC ok)

You will need to apply online through the company website.

Agent Methods: https://www.agentmethods.com/openings Agent Methods handles insurance website creation and maintenance. They offer a "part-time customer support representative" job whose general hours are 9am to 12pm Eastern time. A successful candidate must be customer service oriented with the ability to effectively handle customer questions and issues. The starting rate of pay is $18 per hour. The applicant is required to answer four questions listed on the site along with a resume and cover letter to the email address provided.

Alorica: https://www.alorica.com/careers/work-at-home/ This company offers award-winning customer experience and call center outsourcing solutions to provide superior business services and exciting career opportunities. A customer support representative has required education, experience, and skills, which are minimal. If you can type, have some customer service skills, and can manage your time, you're likely to get through. The equipment is what can be the challenging part.

Alorica's equipment qualifications are below:

- Laptop or desktop 3 years or newer
- Intel i3 core processor
- High-speed internet access / 2MBP download minimum
- Monitor 17" or larger
- Windows 10
- 2GB ram or more

- Processor speed of 1GHZ on multi-core processor or 1.4 GHz on single-core processors
- Minimum graphic resolution: 1024X768
- Sound card with speakers
- Internet connection: DSL, cable, or fiber optic
- Headset

Equipment and Internet speed qualifications may vary depending on client needs.

American Express:

https://jobs.americanexpress.com/jobs?keywords=virtual%20home%20based%20work%20from%20home&page=1 Who hasn't heard of American Express? They're one of the oldest, most established credit card companies. When I did my search, there was no work from home jobs available, but they do come up and are customer service or technical in nature.

Anthem:

https://anthemcareers.ttcportals.com/search/jobs/in?cfm10=&location=&page=1&q=remote# Anthem is a provider of health insurance in the United States and is the largest for-profit managed health care company in the Blue Cross/Blue Shield Association. The remote positions offered on the career site give the option of office-based or remote. Roles include audit and reimbursement, RN clinician, QI specialist, and other highly qualified professional jobs for the healthcare and insurance specialist.

Appen: https://appen.com/jobs/part-time-jobs/ Appen provides or improves data used for the development of machine learning and artificial intelligence products. Appen only offers jobs that can be done from home. The types of jobs included are micro-tasks, projects, or surveys, and data collection. After you choose a type of job, your email is confirmed, and then you register and get started right away. This site can be used by pretty much anyone, little to no experience required for many of the positions, with no equipment requirements. The downside is that you will either be performing micro tasks for very little pay per task or have to pass a comprehensive assessment test that can be very difficult.

Asurion:
https://careers.asurion.com//ListJobs?CloudSearc hValue=remote&prefilters=none&CloudSearchLoca tion=none Asurion is a leading provider of device insurance, warranty, and support services for cell phones, consumer electronics, and home appliances. They offer a

"Remote Technician, Customer Care Representative" job. The customer care representative requires open scheduling flexibility, 6 months customer service experience, ability to pass technical readiness assessment, ability to pass background and drug screen.

The physical equipment requirements are:

- Distraction-free environment
- High-speed internet service (does not specify the speeds or if it must be hardwired)
- Computer with Windows 7 or better
- Asurion supplies the phone equipment.

Blackboard:

https://careers.blackboard.com/careers Blackboard is an educational technology company with corporate headquarters in Washington, DC. It is known for Blackboard Learn, a learning management system. They currently offer a bilingual customer service specialist, customer success advisor position.

Equipment qualifications:

- Quiet workspace
- DSL or cable internet
- Internet speed with download 10Mbps and upload 5Mbps
- Ping of less than 100 ms

Blooms Today:

https://www.bloomstoday.com/careers/independent-sales-representative Blooms Today is an online retail florist. They offer an "Independent Sales Representative" position, which is open to all states except for Texas, California, and Florida. This is a sales position, so there needs to be a sales-minded mentality in place with a drive and comfort in making sure to convert calls to sales. You will need to have either experience in sales or an interest in working in sales. The post states that the average pay for an independent sales rep is $15 per hour, with top-performing reps making an average of $24 per hour.

Physical equipment specifications:

- 2.1 GHz processor
- RAM – minimum 4 GB
- Windows 7 or better
- Monitor

- VOIP phone
- Wired USB headset
- Current and valid antivirus software

Brighten Communications:

https://www.brightenemployment.com/CallerInfo.aspx Brighten Communications is a business-to-business telemarketing company specializing in the outsourcing of lead generation. They offer a "Caller" position. The site states that this is a calling job where the candidate makes lead generation calls on behalf of various clients. The hours to be worked are Monday through Thursday from 8 am to 5 pm west coast time. You can work from 20-33 hours per week, depending on your stats and company workload. Starting pay is $12 per hour while learning the online system. The position is a 1099 independent contractor position paid weekly. The only equipment requirements that are specified are high-speed internet and a working home phone line.

Broadpath: http://www.broad-path.com/join-our-team/careers/ This company provides specialized business, compliance, and technology services to healthcare payers and providers in commercial and government sectors.

These are the types of jobs they had posted for work from home:

- health insurance claims auditor
- workforce manager
- call center RN
- claims processor
- provider enrollment analyst
- provider credentialing analyst
- medical review RN
- bilingual customer service representative

CACI International:

https://careers.caci.com/ListJobs?location=remote & CACI International Inc. provides services to many branches of the US federal government, including defense, homeland security, intelligence, and healthcare. CACI offers professional jobs requiring the successful candidate to have experience in the field of their role and experience working with government entities such as NASA.

Some of the job titles currently being sought after are:

- contract administrator

- voice and network engineer
- field service representative
- telecommunications analyst

Clevertech:

https://www.clevertech.biz/careers#Jobs Clevertech uses digital innovation to solve real-world challenges, backed by 18 years' experience and a professional, solution-focused team of engineers. This site hosts a collection of remote software job opportunities.

Roles include:

- ruby/react software engineer
- MuleSoft developer
- product/visual designer
- react native developer
- other professional software jobs

Concentrix:

https://careers.concentrix.com/work-at-home Concentrix brings together unmatched talent and all the tools and capabilities to power the greatest customer engagement. They are hiring a "Sales and Customer Service

Representative" but only in select states (AL, AR, AZ, CO, DE, FL, GA, IA, ID, IN, KS, KY, LA, MI, MN, MS, MO, NC, ND, NH, NM, NV, OH, OK, PA, SC, SD, TN, TX, UT, VA, VT, WI, WV, and WY). The positions require strong customer service skills, computer and internet savvy, with the ability to operate several applications at once, and open schedule availability. The equipment specifications are vague; instead, the site instructs the applicant to hold off on purchasing any equipment until a job offer is extended. High-speed internet is, of course, required, but again, the exact speeds are not indicated.

Conduent:

https://jobs.conduent.com/careers/jobs?keywords= &page=1 Conduent delivers mission-critical services and solutions on behalf of businesses and governments. Most of the jobs listed were posted for the in-office positions, but there was a virtual customer experience associate posting and a virtual senior software quality assurance tester.

Crowdstrike:

https://www.crowdstrike.com/careers/ This is a cybersecurity technology company that provides endpoint security, threat intelligence, and cyberattack response services. I found 64 total results for remote jobs with crowdstrike. They are all very technical, requiring a high degree of skill and education. The most recent remote job postings are Sr. UX designer, Sr. data engineer, Sr. manager platform security, and other specialized roles.

Datastax:

https://www.datastax.com/company/careers They describe themselves as the company behind the massively scalable, highly available, cloud-native NoSQL database built on Apache Cassandra. The company's career site boasts that they are on the 2019 flexjob list of top companies to watch for remote jobs. Being that the company has such a specific specialty, expect to need to have very selective experience and education.

Dell: https://jobs.dell.com/category/remote-jobs/375/56067/1 Dell is an American multinational computer technology company that develops, sells, repairs, and supports computers and related products and services. There is a large variety of positions open with Dell, including sales, a threat hunter, data engineer, and director of advanced analytics.

Direct Interactions:

https://www.directinteractions.com/careers/ We

handle customer-obsessed organizations to deliver outstanding customer calls with our highly-skilled, emotionally intelligent, US-based agents. The positions offered here are 1099 contract positions paying $10-$12 per hour. The qualifications they are looking for are basic customer service and technical skills. For equipment, you will need hard-wired internet, landline telephone service, client-specific USB headset, and a PC computer (not a Mac) with antivirus and malware/spyware installed.

Ellucian: https://www.ellucian.com/about-us/careers Ellucian powers higher education with innovative, industry-exclusive technology. They offer Senior Colleague HR Consultant, Senior Programmer Analyst, and CRM Recruit jobs.

Frontline: https://www.frontlineeducation.com/about/careers/#career-iframe Serving the education community with integrated tools, best practices, and caring people to support their pursuit of excellence. They are hiring a services consultant, K-12, and a services consultant K-12 special education

GDIT:

https://www.gdit.com/careers/search/?q=remote

General Dynamics Information Technology are the people supporting some of the most complex government, defense, and intelligence projects across the country. There are many remote positions available. You will need to be highly technically skilled, and either already have military clearance or the ability to obtain it. The roles that GDIT is recruiting for are solutions architect, network engineer, ETL programmer, a testing engineer with secret clearance, technical program manager, and many others.

HSN (Home Shopping Network):

https://jobs.hsn.com/search-jobs/home/565/1 HSN, formerly Home Shopping Network, is an American free-to-air television network that offers deals and special values every day. They offer part-time work at home as a customer order specialist. This position is available only in Florida and Tennessee. Within each state, employment is only offered in certain counties. The employee must have a home office set up to include a computer, landline, phone, and high-speed internet. The exact specifications are not listed, but the post does state that most home computers and bundled services will comply with requirements. After the interview is when a detailed list of the specific equipment needed is provided.

The pay rate is $11.50 per hour with an increase every 3 months for the first year and then an automatic increase every 6 months.

Humana: https://www.humana.com/careers
Humana Inc. is a for-profit American health insurance company based in Louisville, Kentucky. This company is ranked 15 by flexjobs as the most flexible employer. There are a huge number of positions posted. The site states that 47% of its staff work remotely over half the time. The positions available included health information consultant, senior medical coding auditor, healthcare training lead, Medicare sales representative, and many more. Each position has different roles, requirements, and qualifications needed.

Infocision:
https://recruiting.adp.com/srccar/public/RTI.home ?c=1154851&d=External-WAH Infocision is the leading provider of direct marketing solutions for numerous companies across a diverse range of industries. There are exactly two jobs listed for the positions available. They are for customer service and sales, both work from home.

The site lists the following requirements to be eligible to work from home:

- PC, Chromebook, or Mac book with a USB port
- Webcam
- USB headset
- High-speed internet
- Must be a permanent resident of one of the following states: Alabama, Colorado, Georgia, Indiana, Kentucky, New Mexico, Mississippi, North Carolina, Ohio, Oregon, Pennsylvania, Tennessee, Texas, and West Virginia

Good for someone just starting up with a minimum investment on equipment if you have internet.

Jack Henry and Associates:
https://careers.jackhenry.com/jobs This company is a provider of technology solutions and payment processing services primarily for the financial services industry.

All the jobs available are very technical in nature:

- senior software engineering manager

- senior iOS mobile engineer
- senior lending product manager
- senior product manager
- systems/network administrator
- cloud solutions architect

JWC Communications LLC:

https://www.jwcworkfromhome.com/job-openings

This company provides quality virtual call center services to its clients by providing them with the professional care they deserve. This company appears to be connected with Arise as a micro virtual call center.

The posted job opportunities are:

- customer sales
- customer service
- inbound collection and sales
- seasonal inbound sales and customer service
- customer service support
- inbound customer service and software tech support
- customer and product support
- inbound customer service calls

All positions are posted as paying $9-$14 per hour and seem to have a dual customer service and sales component.

Kaplan Inc:

https://ghc.wd1.myworkdayjobs.com/KTP_Careers/2/refreshFacet/318c8bb6f553100021d223d9780d30be Kaplan is an American for-profit company that provides educational services to colleges and universities and corporations and businesses, including higher education programs, professional training and certifications, test preparation, and student support services. Most of the jobs posted were a little dated (over 30 days old), and they were all education-related, so you will need to have some educational background and from the jobs posted, it seems to be mostly a nursing and medical centered education that is needed.

Kellyconnect:

https://kellyconnectjobs.force.com/s/jobsearch KellyConnect partners with industry innovators for brand advocacy, customer service, technical support, and value-added sales. The most current job openings are for chat technical support representatives, technical support representatives, and account, billing, and technical support representatives. These might be good jobs for beginners with minimal requirements and experience needed for the support reps. The site says that the pay starts at $13.00 per hour with a $1.00 increase after 90 days.

Lionbridge: https://careers.lionbridge.com/home
Lionbridge Technologies, Inc is an American company that provides localization and AI training data services.

They offer the following remote jobs:

- mobile and desktop internet search reviewer
- online maps quality analyst
- personalized ads evaluator
- personalized internet assessor
- social media assessor

Most of the positions require that you have a good grasp of tech and the internet. Basic equipment requirements are a laptop and an Android device with dependable internet. The time commitment for most positions is 10-20 hours per week.

Liveops:
https://join.liveops.com/careers/?_ga=2.1820017.11

41236801.1585255337-1279460694.1574353906&utm_source=apexbar&utm_medium=notification&utm_campaign=apexbar#jobs-listing This is a cloud call center company based in Scottsdale, Arizona. As an online call center, this site had listings for a remote work from home independent contractor, a remote work from home call center representative, and a remote work from home independent contractor (licensed insurance agent).

McKesson Corporation:
https://mckesson.wd3.myworkdayjobs.com/External_Careers/1/refreshFacet/318c8bb6f553100021d223d9780d30be This is an American company distributing pharmaceuticals and providing health information technology, medical supplies, and care management tools. The work from home opportunities mostly specified what state the individual needed to be in while working remotely. Positions range from account executive in Minnesota to primary care account executive in Alabama, to a field service representative in South Carolina.

Nexrep: https://nexrep.com/marketplace/ Nexrep is an outsourced contact center offering services leveraging a highly-skilled, dedicated, certified, flexible, US-based agent network. This site did not have a job listings page. Instead, because it is essentially a work from home call center, it immediately directs you through to their 'marketplace registration,' which will guide you through a 20-minute process, and then you will receive follow up calls and emails.

nThrive: https://careers-nthrive.icims.com/jobs/search?pr=0&searchLocation=12781--Remote&schemaId=&o= From patient-to-payment, nThrive provides all the technology advisory expertise, services, analytics, and education programs health care organizations need to thrive in the communities they serve. The only job listed currently is the cancer registry abstractor. Requirements for this position are very specific, referring to the cancer registry, medical knowledge, and experience with various electronic medical record systems.

Omni Interactions: https://omniinteractions.applicantpro.com/jobs/ All the positions with this company are work from home jobs. Most of the positions have minimum experience required, so this is a great place for beginners and people looking for steady schedules. Pay starts at $13 per hour. You are required to complete a computer speed test and post your computer specifications via a screenshot.

The site also lists all the physical requirements that your home office will have to have:

- Minimum internet speed of 50 Mbps download and 10 Mbps upload
- Ethernet connection only
- Noise-canceling USB headset
- Webcam
- Google chrome
- Minimum of 1.6 GHz/2GB Ram/ 40 GB Free Space
- Dual monitors
- Flexible schedule to accommodate full or part-time including weekends and training is done as full-time hours
- Enclosed space in the home that is noise-free and has a closed door
- Type minimum of 35WPM
- Ability to navigate a computer and move between multiple screens

Onesupport:

https://onesupport.com/onesupport-careers/ This company offers the best in full home technology services with OneSupport. This is more than just software and full home computer and device support, it's a team of trained and talented on-demand technology advisors.

They offer Business Customer Care Representative, Customer Care Representative, and Technical Support Representative positions. Qualifications are easy to meet. The candidate must speak and write well, be able to type, and have some tech knowledge.

The equipment requirements:

- Internet speed of at least 2 MBPS download and 1 MBPS upload
- Windows 8.1 or 10
- Processor specifications
- Direct or wired internet connection
- Skype compatible USB headset
- 15" or larger monitor, preferably two
- Webcam

The customer care position was posted at $10 per hour with some benefits available and looks like some sales component.

Paragon planners:

https://paragonplanners.com/employment/ Paragon planners specializes in appointment setting, territory management, event planning, marketing, virtual assistants, and sales support. They are hiring Regional Schedulers. The qualified applicant will be making calls to set appointments for their assigned client. They will need to be able to make 18-20 calls per hour, setting 10-18 appointments per week, depending on the client's specifications. The work hours are 8:30-4:30 Monday to Friday, and the pay starts at $12-14 per hour, depending on experience. The candidate will need to have customer service skills, communication capabilities, and be able to navigate Windows and email applications.

The physical equipment requirements:

- Dedicated phone line or VOIP
- Windows 7 or up
- No Macs or tablets
- 2GB memory
- 2.0 GHz processor
- Current antivirus and anti-spam ware

PATLive: https://www.patlive.com/careers/ With PATLive, you'll never miss a call and always provide great customer service. They offer message taking., boast they are 100% US-based, have after-hours call coverage, and appointment scheduling. They are hiring English or Spanish speaking remote call center agents. Eligible candidates must reside in Florida or Georgia. The pay starts from $12-14, depending on the shift.

Perficient: https://www.perficient.com/careers Perficient is the leading digital consultancy, transforming how the world's biggest brands connect with customers and grow their businesses. The remote roles listed on the career page are numerous and are all highly technical in nature. Some of the position titles include healthcare azure technical architect, data engineer, salesforce B2B commerce developer, and many others.

Prudential: https://jobs.prudential.com/job-listing.php?keyword=remote&jobType=&location=&jobLabel=&jobLocation= Prudential Financial, Inc. is an American Fortune Global 500 and Fortune 500 company whose subsidies provide insurance, investment management, and other financial products and services to both retail and institutional customers throughout the United States and in over 40 other countries. They are hiring Senior learning specialists, internal wholesalers for life insurance, and a senior learning specialist team coach for the center of excellence.

Salesforce:

https://www.salesforce.com/company/careers/ Most of the remote jobs were 30 days or older, but there is a variety of jobs available, mostly executive-level positions.

SAS global solutions:

https://sasglobalsolutions.com/apply-now SAS Global Solutions, LLC is a virtual service corporation that offers customer service professionals the opportunity to work from home taking inbound calls for customer service, sales, and technical support roles. To apply for a work from home position, you are automatically directed to a remote work application. The application does not state what skills, qualifications, or experience the company is looking for in a candidate. However, it does state that the employee is a 1099 contractor, there is a $9.99 fee to conduct a background check, and that the candidate will have a virtual office with at least Windows 8, a headset, and high-speed internet before the end of training to be able to begin working.

Secure Work: https://jobs.dell.com/search-jobs/remote/375-30225/1 This company is a United

States-based subsidiary that provides information security services, protecting its customers' computers, networks, and information assets from malicious activity such as cybercrime. A Dell company, the remote career site included positions with VMWare, Dell Technologies, and Secureworks. All positions are very specialized and uniquely qualified with roles such as software engineer, senior cloud integration engineer, and senior security researcher.

Sedgwick:
https://recruiting.adp.com/srccar/public/RTI.home?d=ExternalCareerSite&c=1137841 Sedgwick's casualty risk solutions are designed to care for your employees and customers, protect your brand, and save you money. One work from home opportunity is listed as a service center associate e-support. The requirements for the position are minimal, with a start pay of $13.00 per hour.

Sitel: https://jobs.sitel.com/job/Virtual-Work-from-Home-Inbound-Call-Center-Associate-Any/512652900/ Sitel is a virtual employee-based team supporting global fortune 500 companies in the insurance, travel and leisure, sport, and telecommuting industries. This is literally a call center from home environment. This is a good place for beginners because not a lot of experience is required.

However, before even taking the required assessments and testing, the company provides a list of essentials you will need to make sure that you have everything they require to get the job done:

- Desktop or laptop
- Windows 10
- All peripherals must be wired
- A separate 19" monitor
- Windows anti-virus
- RAM – 4gb
- Processor speed – 2Ghz or more
- 3 available USB ports
- Internet speed – download 5MB. Upload speed 3MB
- ISP highly stable and latency over 100ms
- DSL or Broadband – no Wi-Fi or hotspots
- Home router with wired link to PC
- Specific noise-canceling headset

Slingshot:

https://apply.workable.com/getslingshot/j/9A6206 93F9/ Slingshot is one of the best Utah startups, and has been recognized by Inc Magazine as one of America's fastest-growing companies. They offer the position of an at-home sales representative. You will need to have at least one-year experience in a call center, sales, or customer service environment.

The physical equipment requirements:

- 2 monitors
- USB headset
- Webcam

Starting pay s $14 per hour plus commission.

Sutherland:

https://www.sutherlandglobal.com/about-us/remote-engagement-for-job-seekers A leading provider of work-at-home solutions, Sutherland Remote Engagement services matches the skills and interests of professionals with the right job opportunities. They offer remote underwriter, customer service consultant chat, customer care support: 60- or 90-day contract, and medical coding associate jobs. For customer care support positions, the candidate will need to have some customer service skills and experience.

Additionally, the physical equipment requirements are:

- 2.0 GHz Dual Core or better processor
- 2 GB Ram
- 10 GB available hard drive space
- Windows 7 at minimum
- Internet – 1Mbps upload and 15Mbps download
- Noise-canceling microphone and headset

Sykes: https://jobs.sykes.com/en-US/page/fp-home The company provides business process outsourcing services, IT consulting, and IT-enabled services, such as technical support and customer service. They have a customer service representative, work from home in Canada. No equipment qualifications or starting wages were listed before the application process could be started, but it did specify that the work from home position was centered in Canada.

Teladoc: https://teladochealth.com/careers/ This is a multinational telemedicine and virtual healthcare company based in the United States. They are hiring a member service representative. You will need to be able to stay HIPPA compliant, with three years of exceptional customer service skills. Some college is required, an associate degree preferred, with a distraction-free workspace in the home and hardwired internet.

Teleperformance: https://careers.teleperformanceusa.com/en-US/page/work-from-home This company is a global leader in digitally integrated business services, with a passion for simpler, faster, and safer interactions.

Transcom: https://na.transcom.com/en/careers-na#open-positions This is a Swedish outsourcing company that provides customer care, sales, technical support, and collections services through an extensive network of contact centers and work-at-home agents. They hire part-time customer service agents, call center team leaders, and technical support advisors.

Ttec: https://www.ttecjobs.com/en/work-from-home Ttec is a global customer experience (CX) technology and services company focused on the design, implementation, and delivery of exceptional CX. While most of the opportunities were for countries outside of the US, there were a couple American based positions: inside sales representative, technical support representative, temporary trainer, and temporary manager.

United Health Group:

https://careers.unitedhealthgroup.com/search-jobs

United Health Group Incorporated is an American for-profit managed health care company based in Minnetonka, Minnesota, and it offers health care products and insurance services. At the time of writing this book, there were 112 jobs available for a specific location or telecommute considered. The positions ranged from a benefit configuration analyst to a licensed chiropractor to a part-time care coordinator.

Unum:

https://unum.wd1.myworkdayjobs.com/External/1/
refreshFacet/318c8bb6f553100021d223d9780d30be

Unum provides supplemental insurance coverage in the workplace. The only remote position at the time of this research was for a bilingual customer service representative.

vidIQ: https://careers.vidiq.com/ vidIQ Vision for Chrome is a suite of powerful tools that every creator needs access to if they want to build their audience on YouTube. On the job board, it states that vidIQ is hiring for a Scala developer, a UI/UIX designer, director of product management, and a copywriter.

Vivint:

https://www.vivint.com/company/careers/team/customer-service Vivint Smart Home, Inc. is an American public smart home company in the United States and Canada. All the positions are state-specific, meaning that even though the role is remote, you must reside in the state that the position is being offered in.

Vmware:

https://careers.vmware.com/main/jobs?page=4&tags=Yes VMware is a global leader in cloud infrastructure and digital workspace technology, accelerating digital transformation for evolving IT environments. The career page allows you to narrow your search to work from home positions. There were 226 jobs available. The site grouped them by experience level. There were 123 business leadership, 101 manager and professional, 1 executive, and 1 internship available. All required high levels of experience and education. The following states have work from home opportunities: Florida, Nevada, and Utah. The positions they are hiring for: customer service-account creation and services, customer solutions tech support, and customer service representative-monitoring specialist.

Wayfair:

https://www.wayfair.com/careers/jobs/?countryIds=7&gh_src=a5f36eaa2 Wayfair is an American e-commerce company that sells furniture and home-goods. The positions listed that Wayfair is hiring remotely for are a learning technologist, inbound sales-agent, and customer service. For the customer service position, the starting pay is $14 per hour, you'll need customer service skills and experience, with a successful tenure at a high-volume environment. Wayfair provides all the equipment and requires that you maintain required internet speeds of 25 Mbps download and 5 Mbps upload with a hard-wired internet connection.

Williams Sonoma: https://wsgc.betterteam.com/ Williams Sonoma Inc. is an American publicly traded consumer retail company that sells kitchen-wares and home furnishings. Customer Service Agent positions are only for people living in the states of Arizona, Nevada, or Florida. The employee takes customer calls regarding the customer's questions and concerns about their order with Williams Sonoma. You will need to have customer service experience, communication, and data entry skills. You must be able to complete a mandatory 3-week training session with 100% attendance. Starting pay is $12 per hour with overtime available.

Working Solutions:

https://jobs.workingsolutions.com/category/work-from-home/ There was not a job posting section. Instead, the site asks that you provide an email with which to sign up for communication. Then, it asks that you select what areas you have an interest in. That would seem to be what jobs are available.

The possibilities listed are:

- contact center customer service
- corporate travel agent
- event ticketing and sales
- healthcare customer service
- hotel booking customer service agent
- insurance customer service agent
- medical billing
- sales and customer service
- seasonal work
- senior living customer care

- travel customer care
- video chat customer service

After you select what areas you have an interest in, then you are to upload a resume and complete a profile to proceed.

World Travel Holdings:
https://worldtravelholdings.com/work-home/ World Travel Holdings offers work at home positions that involve selling and servicing fabulous cruise and resort vacations for more than 40 top travel brands while building customer loyalty. The only requirements listed are that you have a private area to work in, free of distractions. They provide the initial setup to include a computer, phone, surge protector, and other optional supplies. There is a $250 deposit for the equipment which comes out of 5 payroll deductions. You will need to already have high-speed internet, 10.0 Mbps download, and 5.0 Mbps upload.

Xerox: https://www.xerox.com/en-us/jobs/work-from-home Xerox offers "workplace solutions, document management, and digital printing technologies to help organizations communicate, connect, and work. Xerox has over 8,000 employees working from home and has been actively creating a remote workplace for over 30 years. The positions they are offering include customer care, technical support, data entry, image tagging, quality control, systems development, software programming, and administrative support.

Chapter 7: Online Gig Work/Freelance Marketplaces

There are some sites dedicated to helping you find online work. Most of these sites will require you to create an online profile, and then prospective employers and employees can interact.

This list is current as of April 2020. Included for each marketplace is a description of the marketplace, a list of pros and cons, and a personal perspective. The description is a direct quote from either the site themselves or another reputable site from the first page from the google site. Similarly, the pros and cons are compilations of listed pros and cons from other sites, users, blogs, and articles detailing each marketplace.

I personally at least visited each site and reviewed the pros and cons described on various websites to give you as much information as possible before you go visit the site because time really is money. I tried to do as much of the heavy lifting for you as possible.

This is sort of a vetting process so that you can make the best decision as quickly as possible. A few blogs and articles that suggested various online marketplaces included sites that either did not exist or were not worth mentioning.

The only sites that were excluded from this list are sites that did not offer the user a way to make money, were more social media in nature, were not a good source of information for freelancers from the United States, were for in-person freelancing and not work from home opportunities, or were an individual attempting to create their own income.

99designs: https://99designs.com/ This is a global creative platform for custom graphic design, logos, websites, and more. It is basically a design contest, where a party submits a request for a design, and then designers who are also using the platform submit a response to the request with their own ideas.

Pros: For the buyers of the designs, they have many affordable options to choose from when they submit their design requests. The designer can choose their projects by only responding to requests that they are interested in or that suit their needs.

Cons: This overly competitive marketplace is a common thread with the online marketplaces for freelancers, 99designs has the same drawback. In order to be able to solicit work, a designer must not only be talented in their design area, but they also have to be able to effectively communicate their design idea in their briefs.

Creative Market: https://creativemarket.com/ This is an online marketplace for community-generated design assets. This is more of an Etsy style of freelancer marketplace where virtual designers showcase their work and sell it on this platform.

Pros: You create your own kind of store, where you build your own shop and showcase your talents. When you sign up, you gain access to others' designs and products as well.

Cons: This is less of a gig seeking, offering site, and more of an online marketplace for design, which is not for everyone. You have to already have an established portfolio or an online presence to even begin the process to become part of the marketplace.

DesignCrowd: https://www.designcrowd.com/ This is an online crowdsourcing platform founded in 2008 that helps startups, businesses, and entrepreneurs connect with a global network of designers. The platform uses three basic dropdown menus - categories, designers, and jobs - to help guide either the designer or the design seeker. Because it is essentially a design contest and there is so much competition, it can be harder to make money.

Fiverr: https://www.fiverr.com/ This site was started in 2010, where all tasks were $5, hence the name "Fiverr." It is a marketplace where you can buy and sell digital services such as content creation, business card templates, and other unique digital services. Buyers are the parties buying the digital service (voiceover, blog post, virtual assistance, etc.), and the Sellers are the parties providing these digital services.

Pros: This is an easy to use platform with smooth navigation for both buyers and sellers. Seller information is easily accessible. The platform allows for ease of communication and flow of information from buyer to seller and vice versa. It provides a large, diverse market in the virtual and the real marketplace.

Cons: It can be an overly competitive marketplace. The Fiverr concept of digital services for $5 hurt the freelancer economy and lowered the standard wage for many services. There are some iffy services and sellers. You get what you pay for. If you are still expecting to only pay $5, then buyer and seller beware.

Freelancer: https://www.freelancer.com/
Freelancer is an online marketplace where one can find and hire top freelancers, web developers, and designers inexpensively. The services and gigs offered seem to be as varied as the word "freelancer" can encompass.

Pros: There is a large variety of tasks to be performed and, therefore, jobs to bid on. The site requires you to choose from a list of possible skillsets so that you can be open to as many opportunities as possible.

Cons: The number of freelancers on the site means that there is so much competition that finding a job and then successfully landing one after bidding can be very difficult. There is a general consensus that there is a lack of communication, and that is hard to reach someone to resolve issues.

Gigster: https://gigster.com/ This is a website that allows users to have tech projects built on demand. This online marketplace is a specialized site looking to match highly skilled developers, designers, and project managers with the world.

Pros: It has a great reputation for providing highly professional, knowledgeable talent with businesses. All of the gigster talent pool has been vetted for excellence in knowledge and skill, and the level of jobs and pay reflects that.

Cons: This may not a good place to start for someone without high-level tech skills. As is true with other freelance online marketplaces, there can be more talent than there are gigs, not allowing for a steady source of reliable income.

Guru: https://www.guru.com/ Guru is one of the best freelance websites to find and hire freelancers online and get work done. Most of the jobs post as available are under the programming and development category. The platform itself is hard to use, which, from the very beginning, poses many problems. There is not a wide variety of tasks or jobs available, nor is it skill specified, so your options and possibilities are greatly narrowed.

HireRemotely: https://hireremotely.co/ This is a global network of top-rated freelancer web and mobile app developers. The scope of work performed is narrowed so that only specific skillsets can register with the site. This site is not beginner-friendly for the freelancer with limited skills or experience

Toptal: https://www.toptal.com/ This platform enables startups, businesses, and organizations to hire freelancers from a growing network of top talent in the world. The platform's emphasis is on the top 3% of the freelancer community with a focus on developers, designers, finance, project managers, and product managers.

<u>Pros:</u> If you are of the top 3%, you will gain access to a higher pay rate than other platforms. There is a rigorous screening and validation process for both freelancers and hiring entities so that the freelancer will deal with top-notch, quality clientele.

<u>Cons:</u> The very rigorous screening process means that if you are still working on your skillset, this higher echelon of payment may not be within your reach. You have to have not only the proper amount of skills but a certain amount of experience to be able to showcase your work and stand out among other applicants. This is not a platform that can generally be utilized by newbie freelancers.

Upwork: https://www.upwork.com/ Upwork connects businesses of all sizes to freelancers, independent professionals, and agencies for all their hiring needs. It could be described as a more sophisticated, pricier, professional version of Fiverr. Their categories of digital professionals range from very technical, skill rich categories such as web, mobile, and software development, IT and networking, data science and analytics, engineering and architecture to more creative, people-related skills such as design and creative, writing, customer service, and sales and marketing.

Pros: Their free membership allows for you to try it out without being financially committed. There are a large number of jobs available.

Cons: You have to pay for "proposals." Proposals act as the bid to work the job from seller to buyer, and you have purchase from a credit system to be able to bid on the job, even though there is no enrollment fee. There is also a significant fee taken from the freelancer to pay Upwork. Upwork offers a tier system that makes the percentage taken from the freelancer to be reduced when the freelancer works with the same client, but that percentage is still significant, considering.

Zirtual: https://www.zirtual.com/ This company offers virtual assistant services for entrepreneurs, professionals, and small teams. This is a member of the startups.co platform, which is a great source of information and guidance for the budding entrepreneur.

Pros: Offers opportunities for college-educated, administrative minded, and experienced individuals who don't necessarily have tech or design abilities. For the freelancer with a higher education, it offers a variety of remote work, often with structured, full-time schedules, which some virtual employees do seek.

Cons: You may be afforded less freedom and flexibility since many of the jobs do require the applicants to adhere to a fixed schedule. If your administrative and customer service skills have all been learned on the job with no documented degree, zirtual is missing out on your expertise.

Chapter 8: Other Home-Based Business Ideas

Working from home does not have to mean being tied to an electronic device many hours per day. The reality is that sometimes it does, but there are a few remote earning possibilities that allow you to earn money from home without being on a computer or the phone. You will still need to interact with technology in some sort of way as most entities use apps to connect with their workers. It all depends on what you can do, what you are willing to do, what resources you do or do not have, and what you can do with what you have.

These jobs will allow you to have your base of operations as your home instead of going to an office. Most times, you will be able to choose how frequently and steadily you want to work. These positions can offer a little more flexibility and freedom, in my opinion, than most other work from home type jobs.

Some of these options are:

- Data collector
- Delivery
- Farmer/flea market
- Mystery shopper
- Pet boarding and care
- Renting your space
- Rideshare

Data collector: A data collector sounds exactly like what it is, someone who collects data. Generally, you will be sent on an assignment from the hiring entity to gather information from a retail store. At the store, you will be expected to obtain data on pricing, shelving, availability, and other variables, record this information, and then send it back in. You will need enough computer and tech-savvy to be able to use whatever app is utilized and a computer to communicate and transmit data.

Who will pay you to collect data:

Retail Data LLC: https://retaildatallc.com/careers/ This position is available in all states, primarily in the major city for that state. You will need to have a GED or high school diploma, a valid driver's license with reliable transportation, and vehicle insurance. Your schedule must allow you to work 15-25 hours per week, using a handheld data collection device to obtain data from major retailers. The role is good for someone who is a self-starter, able to move around with ease, sometimes standing on your feet for long periods of time, and tech-savvy enough to use the handheld device to collect the data and a computer to transmit the collected information.

Westat: https://fig.westat.com/ The data collector position is a little different for this employer. Their site shows that they are currently recruiting for several different projects. Each project's data collection position compiles different types of information in various settings, using different methods. There is a project to do medical records abstracting for DAWN (Drug Abuse Warning Network), education and testing assessment for NAEP (National Assessment of Educational Programs), information collection for PATH (Population Assessment of Tobacco and Health), and a project for NOPUS (National Occupant Protection Use Survey). Each project has different tasks, responsibilities, and requirements and is available for different time periods.

Delivery or Shopping: Whether you are delivering groceries, a pizza, or a bottle of wine, delivery jobs are all basically the same. The deliverer (you) picks up an item from a restaurant or store and delivers the item to the customer. These jobs allow you to pick and choose when you work, where you deliver, and how often you work. Unlike a regular delivery job where you have to commit to a schedule, these roles will allow you some of the same autonomy and freedom as other work from home opportunities.

Different apps have different requirements for you and your delivery vehicle, but they are all basically the same – sign into the app, make the deliveries, and get paid about once per week.

- Postmates - https://postmates.com/
- Doordash - https://www.doordash.com/

- Ubereats – https://www.ubereats.com/
- Instacart - https://www.instacart.com/
- Shipt - https://www.shipt.com/
- Grubhub - https://www.grubhub.com/
- Saucey - https://www.saucey.com/
- Caviar - https://www.trycaviar.com/apply
- Deliv - https://www.deliv.co/

Farmer's Market or Flea Market Booth: If you have a small garden at your house and want to sell the excess produce, you can take it to your local farmers market to earn some extra income. Farmer's markets also have products for sale, jams, jellies, homemade products, and other various sundries.

Locate a farmer's market close to you, go check it out in person, find the individual you are to work with to bring your product to market, and go from there.

https://www.localfarmmarkets.org/

https://www.ams.usda.gov/local-food-directories/farmersmarkets

https://www.farms.com/agriculture-apps/technology/farmers-market-locator

The same concept applies to the flea market scenario. Whatever products, supplies, clothing, crafts, etc. that you have at home and want to turn into cash, try a local outdoor (flea) market.

https://fleamarketzone.com/

http://www.fleamarketfinder.org/

http://americanfleas.com/

http://peepawpicker.com/locator/

Mystery Shopper: A mystery shopper is a paid consumer who goes into a store, establishment, business, or wherever they are assigned to go to collect information on their experience with that entity. Their mission is to go in, observe, interact, and report back.

For example, I did a mystery shopper gig awhile back. I was hired by Company A to investigate how all their apartment leasing agents were performing. For this job, I had to make recorded calls to each of the apartment properties. I was scoring each call on a list of criteria such as, "Did they answer with their first name and the name of the property?" and so on. Then, I went in person to these same properties and did the same in person.

Every business that hires mystery shoppers will have different qualifiers, tasks, and things to look for depending on the assignment, the timeframe, and the client.

https://www.marketforce.com/become-a-mystery-shopper

https://multi-value.com/

https://www.secretshopper.com/

https://callcenterqa.org/employment/

https://www.skilcheck.com/mystery-shoppers

Pet Boarding and Care: Do you have a reciprocal love vibe with animals? Turn it into some cash by caring for other people's pets. Tasks you could do might be walking the dog, keeping the cat while they're away, feeding the animal, or giving a pet a bath. Most of the sites are geared towards dogs as they seem to need more intense, personalized, consistent care. Pet walking, boarding, pet sitting, drop-in pet visits, pet daycare, and pet grooming are among the tasks you can take on to earn money from home. All these services have been turned into money-making opportunities for those animal lovers out there.

https://www.rover.com/

http://www.dogwalker.com/

https://www.petbacker.com/

https://petsitter.com/

https://outugo.com/

Renting your space: Boarding houses started the trend of renting out one's personal space as a way of earning money a long time ago. This trend continues today, in so many ways. Whether you have an RV for rent, an extra bedroom, a garage, office space, or even just a parking space outside, there is a way to rent that out to someone who needs to make use of it. You will need to interact with a website or an app to become vetted (verified) and to meet/attract your clientele. The actual work involved will be in maintaining and cleaning the space and in interacting with the individuals renting out your space.

https://www.airbnb.com/

https://www.peerspace.com/

https://www.storeatmyhouse.com/

https://www.neighbor.com/

https://www.spacer.com/

https://www.justpark.com/

https://www.homeaway.com/

Rideshare: The modern-day taxi is the rideshare concept. In case you haven't heard of Uber, this is how it works. Someone logs onto a rideshare app to request a ride from place A to place B. You, the driver, being also logged into that app, pick up that person, drop them off at their destination, and then get paid for it via the app. If you have a newer vehicle, a valid driver's license, vehicle insurance, enjoy driving, and have a personality that will allow you to deal with all walks of people in a variety of scenarios, then this could be a money-making venture for you. This type of work is not for everyone, but it can provide another source of income that doesn't involve going into an office or having to adhere to a schedule other than the one you create for yourself.

https://www.uber.com/

http://lyft.com/

There are other rideshare companies available, but they are more of a pay per ride carpooling service and only available in certain cities. Check some of these other sites to see if you can use them in your area:

https://gocurb.com/

http://www.alvia.com/summon-rideshare/

https://www.flywheel.com/

Chapter 9: 6 Ways to Make Money with Amazon

Amazon is such a Goliath of a company that it needs its own section on the many ways you can make money with Amazon.

1. Sell on Amazon

https://sell.amazon.com/beginners-guide.html

Educate yourself on everything you will need to know to become a seller on Amazon. On the link above, you can learn:

- how to list products
- the importance of the product detail page and how to create yours
- product fulfillment (delivery) options
- learning how to monitor and make use of your performance metrics
- growth opportunities

Amazon Accelerator

You could also sell under the Amazon Accelerator program. Basically, the product manufacturer sells their product exclusively on Amazon. When participating in the Amazon Accelerator program, the seller receives onboarding support, marketing tools, and a venue to test new products, and can solicit feedback to improve the product/process.

Amazon Handmade

You can also sell on Amazon Handmade https://sell.amazon.com/programs/handmade.html

. If you are an artist with handmade crafts to sell, Amazon wants to partner with you. It can be pretty much anything that is handcrafted except for digital products, food, or electronics. The professional selling plan is $39.99 per month. Amazon waives this fee for the Amazon artisan and instead takes a 15% referral fee.

Professional Services

You could sell your professional services on Amazon https://sell.amazon.com/programs/professional-services.html. Amazon Home Services provides Amazon customers with access to service professionals who can help them with various home needs.

Amazon uses the example of a customer purchasing a garbage disposal through Amazon. When the purchase is made, the website will automatically ask the customer if they would like an Amazon Home Service professional to come to install the disposal. Once the request is made, the service request is then routed to a service professional who is registered with Amazon.

To be a home service professional with Amazon, the individual must pass a background check, have proper licensing and authorization depending on the service being offered, and carry the appropriate insurance coverage.

B2B Sales

You could sell on Amazon business https://sell.amazon.com/programs/amazon-business.html. Business to business sales are another of Amazon's many ventures. One business cannot function without interacting with another. The Amazon Business program allows sellers to sell from one business to another, optimizing on such benefits as quantity pricing, business pricing, and other tools to help reach the business your company needs to interact with.

As a business seller, you have the option of selling only to other businesses or to both businesses and consumers. The fee for selling on Amazon as a business is the same as a professional seller - $39.99 a month, along with other referral fees.

Sell Apps on Amazon

You could sell your apps on Amazon https://developer.amazon.com/. This is way out of my league, so I will directly quote exactly what Amazon has to say about how to sell your apps with them.

For Amazon Alexa: "Build natural voice experiences that offer customers a more intuitive way to interact with technology."

Amazon Appstore: "Develop Amazon apps and games for Amazon Fire TV, Fire tablet, and mobile platforms."

Amazon Dash Replenishment: "Build Amazon reordering experiences into your devices."

AWS Developer Center: "Find tools, documentation, and sample code to build applications in your favorite language."

From the sell your apps FAQ supplied by Amazon, an oversimplified explanation of the process on how to sell your apps. Make sure your app meets the specified requirements and guidelines. Pre-test your app. Then, submit your app to the Amazon Appstore.

Sell Your Self-Authored Books

Self-publish with Amazon https://kdp.amazon.com/en_US/. There are some options to self-publishing with Amazon, and Amazon gives you the tools to be able to do so.

1. Publish your digital book with Kindle Direct Publishing. You could earn royalties of up to 70%. You can publish in minutes and have the book appear on Amazon sites within two days. It will make your text available on all Kindle devices and reading apps.

2. Publish your audiobook with ACX (Audiobook Creation Exchange). You could earn high royalties on exclusive or non-exclusive distribution. You can sell on audible.com, amazon.com, and iTunes. You gain easy access to narrators and studio professionals

Sell Your Designs on Merch by Amazon

https://merch.amazon.com/ As an artist, you can sell your designs to Amazon, putting your designs out into the world with no investment or upfront costs and earn a royalty from every purchase made. The customer goes to the page, designs their T-shirt, uses your design, you get paid, and get recognition. Because Amazon has been flooded with content creators sending in their creations, it operates on an invite-only system. You will need to send in a submission of your artwork. Once there is space available, and Amazon has an interest, they will send you an invitation to become an Amazon Merch creator.

This is the simplified process, as Amazon explains, is:

- Upload your custom artwork
- Set the listing price
- Amazon will print what is sold on the T-shirt
- Product gets shipped
- You earn monthly royalties

2. Become an Amazon Affiliate

Become an Amazon Affiliate https://affiliate-program.amazon.com/. As covered previously in this book, an affiliate is an individual or business who earns a commission from selling another's products. This can be done by including links to the products you wish to sell in blog topics, on websites, on a YouTube channel, however you are able to reach a buying audience that will click on the link and make a purchase through your affiliate link, thereby earning you a commission from that sale.

Amazon offers these three simple steps for their affiliate program:

Join for free.

You can join for free, but in order to be approved to be an authentic Amazon affiliate, you must submit an application to the associates team. On the application, you will need to show that you have a way to sell the Amazon products. You will need either a website that you own, your own mobile app, or an acceptable social media group/page.

Advertise with Amazon tools.

After you choose whatever products you want to market to your audience, Amazon will provide linking tools to help you advertise and monetize your site.

Earn money.

The percentage you will earn will depend on the product you have chosen to advertise for Amazon. There is also a bounty program where you can refer consumers to an Amazon program and service and earn a flat fee rather than a percentage.

3. Deliver Amazon Packages

You can either do that as an individual delivering packages, or you can start your own delivery business using Amazon's technology and logistics. As an individual, sign up for Amazon Flex https://flex.amazon.com/. As an independent contractor, you download the app, pick up the block of time that you would like to work, work the agreed-upon shift, and earn your money. Sometimes there are tips from customers to help supplement your earnings.

Because you are an independent contractor, you are responsible for all mileage, gas, parking, and tolls. On the site, Amazon states that they will always pay you $15-19 per scheduled hour. After gas and other factors, you can still earn a decent wage.

4. Become an Amazon Influencer

https://affiliate-program.amazon.com/influencers The influencer program is similar to the affiliate program in the sense that you are earning a commission for every product that is sold through your link. The difference is that for the influencer program, you must have an established, high volume social media presence through either YouTube, Facebook, Twitter, or Instagram. Once you have been established as having a qualifying social media presence, then you can begin the process of being an Amazon Influencer.

Here is how it works:

- You create your storefront with a custom URL and use it to recommend products.
- Share the products with your custom URL
- Earn money when a consumer makes a purchase through your URL

5. Create Videos for Prime Video Direct

https://videodirect.amazon.com/ Prime Video Direct is the delivery platform Amazon uses to push out the films and videos sold by Amazon. According to Amazon, Prime Video

Direct helps rights holders, from independent filmmakers to direct studios, reach Amazon global audiences across hundreds of devices with the same distribution options and delivery quality available to major motion picture and television studios.

This is how you are able to earn income with your videos:

- Flexibility in earning options. Royalties can be earned based on the number of hours content is being streamed, revenue share from rentals, purchases, and monthly channels, ad impressions, or any combo of those options.

- Massive reach. Your content can be found through Prime Video in the US and other areas via any supported device

- Earning optimization. Performance metrics are tracked and can be utilized to optimize how you offer and promote your content

6. Work for Amazon Mechanical Turk

https://www.mturk.com/worker Amazon Mechanical Turk is a crowdsourcing website for businesses to hire remotely located "crowdworkers" to perform discrete on-demand tasks that computers are currently unable to do. Similar to Lionbridge or Appen, this micro-worker opportunity is run by Amazon and can be a good way to earn some extra money from home.

Some of the tasks available to do as an M-Turk worker are:

- Image or video processing. This is really hard for machines to do but easy for humans. You may be tagging an image to optimize advertising, or selecting the best picture to represent a product, or moderating content uploaded by users, or using satellite imagery to identify and classify images.

- Data verification and clean up by finding duplicate entries and verify item details

- Information compilation by answering questions about any topic.

- Filling out surveys.

- Content writing for websites.

- Locating specific fields in large documents.

- Data processing.

- Transcribing and editing audio.

- Translating from one language to another.

- Reviewing the accuracy of search engine results.

Chapter 10: Frequently Asked Questions About Working from Home

If you have never worked remotely in any capacity, you may have a lot of questions or concerns.

The following list of commonly asked questions is in no particular order.

How does your employer know when you're working?

If you are a remote worker who is on the phones or any other hourly position, you are monitored in some type of way to make sure that you are on task and presently working. If your work is by task, such as transcription, writing, or marketing, then the only person that needs to know that you are working is you because the only person you hurt by saying you are working and then not doing so is you.

Do you get distracted?

Absolutely. Every day, all day, in many ways. The challenge is to avoid distractions to begin with. Create an environment where they no longer exist. Then, develop a method of dealing with the distractions quickly and firmly.

What kind of hours do you work?

That's up to you and your situation. I have terrible internet, so I cannot work a traditional remote call center job. That means that there are times that I work from 10pm-2am, or I work 9am-4pm, it's up to me. Plenty of jobs, especially those involving any sort of customer service, will have very structured schedules and, for the most part, are done during normal operating hours.

Can I do other non-work-related tasks while working remotely?

Again, this is person and situation specific. If you are being monitored by a webcam and logged into a system to take calls all day, then no, you cannot. It would be the same as a regular office environment. Breaks would have to be accounted for and taken when appropriate. For others, like myself, you can do what you want, when you want, but be careful that you don't let the whole day get away from you with non-work-related tasks.

Do you get lonely?

Sometimes I will think I miss being around lots of other people, and then I do get around them and remember the value of my own company. In all seriousness, this is another factor to take into consideration. If you are an extreme extrovert and need social time, make sure that you build that into your working plan. Self-care is important to be successful in anything that you do.

What is the biggest challenge when working from home?

The first major challenge is identifying and then locating the job. What are your skills, what are you qualified to do, can you get sufficient internet, what equipment do you have, do you have proper space, and so on.

Another challenge is the work-life balance. When they are both taking place in the same space, it is so easy to let one take over the other.

How fast is remote work growing?

Exponentially, every day, the remote workforce is growing. Before February 2020, there were already projections that the workforce would be equal by 2025 with half on-site and half remotely. Those numbers have skyrocketed recently. I believe that the face of the traditional workforce has changed. Going forward, businesses will adapt to allowing workers to complete their jobs remotely.

How do I get myself ready to work from home?

Treat it like an on-site position as much as possible. Create a distraction-free space and a working schedule so that you can maintain work-life balance and be as productive and happy as possible. Life in your pajamas with no schedule or commitments sounds good until you find yourself having done nothing but chill for almost a week straight and realize your bills are coming due.

Can my kids be home with me while I am working?

Of course, they're your babies. Depending on how old they are and what level of care they need, you may need to have someone there with you to care for them in a separate space in the house or take them to a childcare setting just as you would if you were working onsite. This decision is highly personal and dependent upon your situation.

Conclusion

A few months ago, I would have said that working from home is not for everyone and would have included myself in that category for many reasons. I honestly miss the physicality of leaving the house, doing my job, and then coming home to my significant other to make me crazier.

Working from home can be rewarding financially, mentally, physically, and spiritually. It all depends on how you look at it and how you choose to handle it.

For anyone brand new to working remotely, I welcome you to the work from home community and wish you the most success. Do your research before starting anything. It will save you a lot of time, effort, money, and frustration.

From me to you, I send lots of love, peace, and well wishes. Be safe out there, my friends, and make the most of today. If this book has helped you, enlightened you, or steered you in the right direction, would you please consider leaving me an honest review online where you purchased this book? Online reviews, as we learned earlier in this book, are important for sales and will help me to continue to write further. I sincerely appreciate your time. Thank you!

Resources

As of May 2020, all information contained within this text is accurate and up to date.

In addition to the links provided throughout the text, the following links were also used to locate various information.

https://realwaystoearnmoneyonline.com/get-paid-to-write/

https://realwaystoearnmoneyonline.com/editing-and-proofreading/

https://www.fundera.com/resources/working-from-home-statistics

https://www.dol.gov/general/aboutdol/history/amworkerintro

https://www.bls.gov/opub/mlr/2016/article/the-life-of-american-workers-in-1915.htm

https://www.businessnewsdaily.com/8156-future-of-remote-work.html

https://www.monster.com/career-advice/article/assessing-your-skills

https://www.careeronestop.org/ExploreCareers/Assessments/skills.aspx

https://www.dayjob.com/identifying-your-skills-254/

https://www.myersbriggs.org/my-mbti-personality-type/mbti-basics/the-16-mbti-types.htm?bhcp=1

https://www.truity.com/test/type-finder-personality-test-new

https://realwaystoearnmoneyonline.com/money-earning-directory/art-illustration/

https://reedsy.com/discovery/blog/get-paid-to-readhttps://realwaystoearnmoneyonline.com/closed-captioning-companies/

https://www.thebalancecareers.com/legitimate-data-entry-jobs-from-home-3542500

https://www.numinix.com/blog/2018/11/05/what-are-the-different-categories-of-e-commerce/

https://www.thepennyhoarder.com/make-money/best-mystery-shopping-companies-to-work/

https://www.rasmussen.edu/degrees/technology/blog/programming-careers-for-coding-connoisseurs/

https://freebiesdealsandsteals.com/home-product-testing-free-products-for-review/

https://www.usertesting.com/be-a-user-tester#collapse1

https://www.lifehack.org/articles/money/15-easy-ways-for-everyone-make-money-with-social-media.html

https://realwaystoearnmoneyonline.com/money-earning-directory/translation/

https://theworkathomewife.com/data-entry-jobs-from-home/

https://realwaystoearnmoneyonline.com/voice-over-jobs/

https://www.swiftsalary.com/get-paid-testing-websites-and-apps/

https://creatoracademy.youtube.com/page/lesson/revenue-basics

https://thinkoutsidethecubiclenow.com/work-from-home-jobs-that-dont-require-hard-wired-internet/

https://www.frugalrules.com/delivery-app-jobs/

https://www.consumer.ftc.gov/articles/0053-mystery-shopper-scams

https://hbr.org/2020/03/15-questions-about-remote-work-answered

Milton Keynes UK
Ingram Content Group UK Ltd.
UKHW020036160724
445683UK00070B/592